Post-Disasters Economic and Financial Trends Across Europe

Serkan Yeşilyurt and Sonat Bayram (eds.)

Post-Disasters Economic and Financial Trends Across Europe

PETER LANG

Berlin · Bruxelles · Chennai · Lausanne · New York · Oxford

Bibliographic information published by the Deutsche Nationalbibliothek
The Deutsche Nationalbibliothek lists this publication in the Deutsche Nationalbibliografie; detailed bibliographic data are available on the Internet at https://dnb.dnb.de.

Library of Congress Cataloging-in-Publication Data
Names: Yeşilyurt, Serkan, 1983- editor | Bayram, Sonat editor
Title: Post-disasters economic and financial trends across Europe / Serkan Yeşilyurt and Sonat Bayram (eds.).
Description: Berlin ; New York : Peter Lang, [2026] | Includes bibliographical references.
Identifiers: LCCN 2025050843 (print) | LCCN 2025050844 (ebook) | ISBN 9783631919156 paperback | ISBN 9783631940259 pdf | ISBN 9783631940266 epub
Subjects: LCSH: Finance--Europe | Disasters--Economic aspects--Europe
Classification: LCC HG186.A2 P67 2026 (print) | LCC HG186.A2 (ebook) | DDC 332.094--dc23/eng/20260311
LC record available at https://lccn.loc.gov/2025050843
LC ebook record available at https://lccn.loc.gov/2025050844

ISBN 978-3-631-91915-6 (Print)
ISBN 978-3-631-94025-9 (ePDF)
ISBN 978-3-631-94026-6 (ePUB)
DOI 10.3726/b23029

Published by Peter Lang GmbH, Berlin, Germany

info@peterlang.com

This publication has been peer reviewed.

www.peterlang.com

Contact for General Product Safety Regulation (GPSR): gpsr@peterlang.com

Contents

Figures

Tables

CHAPTER 1

The Rise of Digital Finance: New Business Models With FinTech

Sonat Bayram

ABSTRACT
The revolutionary effects of digital banking and financial technology (FinTech) on the global financial ecosystem are examined in this chapter, with a focus on how they promote economic resilience in the wake of disasters. Financial intermediation has been redefined by technological innovation, especially the incorporation of blockchain, artificial intelligence (AI), big data analytics, and mobile platforms. This has made financial intermediation more efficient, accessible, and inclusive. The paper emphasizes how digital finance accelerated the adoption of contactless payments, robo-advisory services, and decentralized finance (DeFi) apps while reducing disruptions during emergencies like the COVID-19 epidemic. Furthermore, the convergence of environmental, social, and governance (ESG)-focused digital solutions and Green FinTech shows how sustainability concerns are becoming more and more integrated into technological finance. While the benefits of digitization include decreased transaction costs, more financial inclusion, and improved banking efficiency, substantial problems remain, particularly in cybersecurity, data governance, regulatory harmonization, and income inequality. The chapter concludes that as digital finance evolves, its success in crafting a more inclusive, transparent, and sustainable global economy is dependent on strong governance frameworks, cross-border regulation, and ongoing innovation guided by resilience and sustainability principles.

Keywords: Green FinTech, ESG, post-disaster resilience, blockchain, artificial intelligence (AI), decentralized finance

Jel Codes: G20, O33

Introduction

Historically, technological innovations have impacted and transformed the financial sector. The digitalization of financial services has been significantly facilitated by the growing use of computers and the advancement of corporate networks since the mid-twentieth century. The speed, security, and accessibility of financial transactions have all drastically changed because of the advancement of internet technology. New business models have been made possible by this process, which has also served as the foundation for financial technology now referred to as "FinTech" (Arner et al. 2015). The term "digital finance" describes a radical shift in the delivery of financial services brought about by technological advancements. FinTech is a broad field that includes anything from robo-advisors to embedded finance models, from mobile payments to blockchain-based cryptocurrencies, with the goal of making financial services quicker, less expensive, and more widely available (Schueffel 2016). These developments, however, should be viewed as a paradigm shift that seeks to transcend the constraints of conventional financial systems as well as technical advancement.

Conventional financial systems have considerable constraints regarding velocity, expense, and accessibility. Banking transactions are generally limited by designated working hours, and transactions performed at physical branches are laborious. The high costs of financial services represent a significant barrier, especially for low-income individuals and small businesses. Furthermore, those residing in isolated areas or with limited access to banking facilities face difficulties in acquiring financial services. These limits clearly highlight the necessity for digital banking solutions to perform financial transactions without temporal or spatial limitations. This scenario not only diminishes processing durations but also substantially decreases expenses and broadens access to financial services (World Bank 2018).

The increasing adoption of mobile technologies and digital platforms has enabled billions of individuals previously excluded from conventional financial institutions to access fundamental financial services. This is a significant advancement leading to increased financial inclusion. The rise of digital money is allowing new business models to emerge. Digital banks are replacing traditional banking methods and eliminating the dependency on physical branches (Param 2020). Open banking applications allow banks to share data with third-party service providers, which in turn encourages the development of new financial products (Gomber et al. 2018). Embedded financial models enable financial services to be embedded in a variety of goods and services. When combined with the potential for intermediary transactions in DeFi, they offer insights into the future directions of digital finance (Dünya 2024). These creative approaches represent a significant transformation in the financial sector. The promise of digital finance facilitates financial services that are swifter, more secure, more accessible, and more economical, while simultaneously expediting the emergence of innovative business models. These advancements signify a change intended to transcend the limitations of conventional financial systems and render financial services accessible to all societal segments.

Digital Finance and FinTech: Key Concepts and Global Trends

The innovative utilization of technology to provide financial services resulted in FinTech. FinTech denotes technological innovations across various sectors, including banking, investment management, insurance, and payment systems. These technologies are intended to facilitate quick, safe, and simple financial transactions (Arner et al. 2015). The fundamental components of FinTech are mobile technology, blockchain, AI, and big data. Distributed ledger technology makes blockchain transactions secure and transparent. Customer service and financial advisory sectors can benefit from machine learning, AI, and fraud detection technologies. Analysis of customer data facilitates the development of customized services and risk management methods through big data analytics. People can access financial services from anywhere at any time because of mobile technologies (Schueffel 2016).

In recent years, the FinTech industry has expanded quickly on a global scale. In 2022, it is projected that global FinTech investments will total $164.1 billion. It ranked third in total investment, although less than the $238.9 billion investments reported in 2022 and 2021 (KPMG 2023). Digital payment systems have significantly impacted FinTech progress. In particular, during the COVID-19 pandemic, contactless payment technology has developed rapidly. These technologies, by eliminating the necessity for face-to-face interaction, have enhanced the safety of purchase. Current forecasts indicate that by 2025, there will be 4.6 billion mobile payment applications worldwide (Statista 2023). By 2027, the global digital payment industry is anticipated to attain $12.55 trillion, expanding at an annual pace of 10%. Digital wallets, wearable technology, QR codes, and contactless payments are significant growth drivers (World Bank 2023).

Consumer innovations are not the primary emphasis of FinTech. It also presents a multitude of chances for enterprises. Financial service automation, for instance, uses the cost advantages of digital platforms to expedite credit applications for small- and medium-sized enterprises (SMEs). Demirgüç-Kunt et al. (2018) state that microfinance services are vital for the growth of the economy, especially in regions without access to the banking system. In addition, open banking laws allow companies to create personalized financial solutions. This allows the financial ecosystem to become more integrated (Gomber et al. 2018). The expansion of DeFi applications is an important trend. These blockchain-based applications allow users to make direct financial transactions without the need for intermediaries. Financial inclusion and the financial sector are undergoing a major change. People who do not have access to the traditional banking system can easily receive basic financial services, such as getting loans and opening accounts through digital finance applications (Schueffel 2016).

In today's world, AI has begun to be used in digital banking, as in every field, to improve user experience. Robo-advisory services automate investment decisions by streamlining investment options and providing customized investment recommendations to clients. Investors are using it easily. The total value of robo-advisors is expected to reach $16 trillion by 2025 (Statista 2023).

The importance of sustainability-focused financial products in the FinTech sector is increasing. Digital financial products that include ESG standards allow investors to make environmentally responsible decisions. Blockchain-based carbon tracking applications have helped companies track their carbon footprints. This is a good development. Thanks to FinTech's environmentally friendly products, both consumers and companies benefit from a more sustainable financial environment (KPMG 2023). FinTech and digital financial services are becoming simpler, more efficient, and more practical, thanks to technological developments. The importance of FinTech in the banking sector will increase due to technological developments.

New Business Models With FinTech: Peer-to-Peer (P2P) Lending, Digital Payments, and the Future of DeFi

The emergence of innovative business models that go beyond traditional financial services is due to the development of FinTech. This section will discuss the innovative business models that are emerging in the digital finance sector.

P2P Lending

P2P lending is a system that allows people to lend directly to each other, bypassing intermediary financial institutions. These platforms connect investors and borrowers, replacing financial intermediation. Platforms like LendingClub assess loan applications and present them to investors, thereby expediting lending processing. Research indicates that P2P lending serves as a vital source of finance, particularly for people and small enterprises lacking access to the banking system (Lenz 2016). The benefits of the P2P lending model encompass minimal transaction expenses, expedited approval procedures, and enhanced accessibility. This model entails both dangers and successes. Elevated default rates, market volatility, and regulatory ambiguities constitute the primary issues confronting P2P lending.

Electronic Payment Systems

E-wallets and mobile payments are significantly improving the economy by speeding up financial transactions. Users can make fast and cost-effective transactions through platforms such as PayPal, Venmo, and WeChat Pay, and the expansion of such systems provides significant convenience for both businesses and individuals. Millions of people in China who do not have access to traditional banking services can manage their money using WeChat Pay and Alipay (Chen & Zhang 2020).

Digital payment systems also have a significant impact on the economy. Studies show that these solutions increase the income of small businesses and enable them to maximize their financial operations. Digital payments are 30% more efficient and more economical. The global digital payment market is expected to reach $12.55 trillion by 2027. This growth will contribute to the development of contactless and mobile payment technologies (World Bank 2021).

Decentralized Finance (DeFi)

DeFi is an ecosystem built on blockchain technology that provides financial services without central authorities. Platforms like Uniswap and Compound allow users to conduct financial transactions without intermediaries. The transparency and accessibility advantages of DeFi have great potential, especially in poor countries. DeFi applications are spreading rapidly. By 2022, assets locked in DeFi applications (TVL) exceeded $70 billion. Nonetheless, several impediments hinder this expansion. Specifically, security risks and legislative ambiguities pose significant challenges to the viability of DeFi. A series of DeFi hacking incidents in 2021 sparked a significant controversy regarding the security of this ecosystem (Wang & Yu 2021). The success of digital finance in the future depends on regulatory frameworks. The European Union's Markets in Crypto Assets (MiCA) policy is designed to ensure that DeFi applications operate in a safer environment. Such rules can protect consumers and, at the same time, encourage the expansion of DeFi (Chen & Zhang 2020).

Solutions Based on AI

Financial advisory and risk management have become much better, thanks to AI, and robo-advisors offer customized portfolio recommendations to investors using algorithms. In this way, investment transactions have begun to automate. Platforms such as Betterment aim to increase returns by optimizing client portfolios, and AI-powered portfolio management outperforms traditional methods (Wang & Yu 2021). Asset management worldwide is also greatly affected by robo-advisory services. On the other hand, AI-driven solutions have become very important in cases such as fraud detection and risk management. Banks can detect potential risks and implement preventive strategies using AI algorithms with big data analytics (Namvar & Naderpour 2018). AI-driven solutions have become the most important way to increase financial inclusion. Microfinance institutions in poor countries evaluate loan applications using AI algorithms and facilitate access to financial services, and thus, these creative ideas stimulate the economy (Chen & Zhang 2020).

Green FinTech and Sustainability

In recent years, financial solutions focused on sustainability have begun to gain prominence in the FinTech sector. Also known as Green FinTech, this topic advocates the development of financial products that comply with ESG criteria. Blockchain-based carbon credit systems and applications that evaluate environmental impacts aid companies in achieving their sustainability goals. Research demonstrates that Green FinTech solutions provide economic benefits for both individuals and businesses. Carbon monitoring solutions allow companies to improve energy efficiency and reduce costs. Furthermore, ESG-oriented digital investment platforms assist users in making ecologically sustainable investment choices (Schueffel 2016).

The Effects of FinTech on Traditional Finance: Transformation of Banks and Advantages of Digitalization

FinTech is revolutionizing traditional banking frameworks through the application of technology in the delivery of financial services. This change is profoundly affecting banks' operations, cost structures, and customer interactions. In response to digitalization, banks are restructuring their corporate operations to provide faster, more economical, and efficient services.

Bank Transformation

The rise of digital banking has significantly changed the business models of traditional banks. Fully digital banks like Revolut, N26, and Monzo have created a new banking paradigm by offering their customers customized services, 24/7 mobile access, and low transaction fees. It has been proven that operating costs are reduced by 60 %–70 % by digital banks (King 2018). Founded in the UK in 2015, Revolut, a digital bank, currently has over 15 million customers. Revolut has reimagined payment systems worldwide with fast transfers, multi-currency accounts, and favorable exchange rates, demonstrating how digital banking impacts the customer experience. Similarly, customers have been able to manage financial transactions more easily, thanks to N26's accessibility and easy-to-use interface (Gomber et al. 2018).

Traditional banks have expedited their digital transformation initiatives to endure this competitive landscape. For instance, major financial institutions like HSBC and Citibank are investing in digitization through AI-enhanced client services, blockchain security solutions, and mobile banking applications. Moreover, several banks seek to provide novel products through partnerships with FinTech firms. Examples of similar efforts include JPMorgan Chase's investments in blockchain technology and Goldman Sachs' digital banking platform, Marcus (Arner et al. 2015). Nonetheless, the emergence of digital banks is amplifying the significance of regulatory frameworks. The European Union's Payment Services Directive 2 (PSD2) rule has facilitated open banking by mandating banks to exchange data with third-party financial service providers. This has enhanced collaborative prospects between FinTech firms and conventional banks, simultaneously fostering rivalry (Demirgüç-Kunt et al. 2018).

Expenditure and Velocity

One of the most apparent impacts of FinTech apps is their substantial reduction of transaction costs. Digitalization has enabled banks to decrease the operational costs of physical branches and expedite transaction times. Online loan application processes are executed 50 % more swiftly than conventional techniques, and transaction expenses are diminished by 30 % (Lenz 2016). Big data analytics and AI technologies are essential for enhancing the operational efficiency of banks. These technologies allow banks to develop more effective strategies by assessing credit risk with more accuracy, detecting fraudulent activities, and predicting consumer behavior. HSBC's fraud detection technology employs big data analytics to proactively identify possible threats, resulting in annual cost savings of millions of dollars for the bank (Schueffel 2016). Digitalization has not only diminished expenses but also accelerated the pace of financial services. Mobile banking software enables customers to execute financial transactions instantaneously. A study in Europe demonstrated that mobile payment solutions are 40% more efficient than conventional payment methods and enhance customer satisfaction (Wang & Yu 2021). In underdeveloped countries that lack access to traditional banking institutions, mobile banking applications have become a vital financial resource. M-Pesa in Kenya demonstrates how digital payment systems work to reduce poverty (Demirgüç-Kunt et al. 2018).

Technology and Security: The Function of Blockchain

Blockchain technology is known as a fundamental element of FinTech applications. Blockchain provides time and cost efficiency, especially in digital payments, asset management, and international transactions. Blockchain-based payment solutions such as Ripple reduce international transfer times from days to seconds. Transaction costs are reduced by 80 % (Gomber et al. 2018). While these developments are taking place, some difficulties prevent the implementation of blockchain technology. Regulatory uncertainties and scalability issues prevent blockchain from being widely implemented in the banking sector. However, due to its decentralized structure, blockchain reduces the risk of fraud and increases transparency in financial transactions. This increases users' trust in blockchain-based services (King 2018).

Client Experience and Customization

FinTech applications have greatly improved the user experience and provided personalized services. AI algorithms analyze consumer spending behavior and provide personalized financial recommendations. Robo-advisory platforms like Betterment aim to improve results by creating portfolios that match investors' risk profiles (Wang & Yu 2021). Personalization goes beyond investment management, and digital banks provide personalized ads and promotions that are informed by consumer behavior. Looking at Revolt's spending statistics helps consumers manage their budgets more effectively. These offerings have increased customer loyalty and allowed banks to get ahead of the competition (Lenz 2016).

Economic and Social Consequences of Digital Finance: Financial Inclusion and Assistance for Small and Medium Enterprises

Digital finance acts as a revolutionary tool that significantly impacts the global economy, affecting both economic and social aspects. Digital finance increases economic potential by improving access to financial services, thereby creating new opportunities for unbanked individuals and SMEs. This section examines the impact of digital finance on financial inclusion and the support it provides to SMEs.

Monetary Inclusion

For individuals who do not have access to the banking system, digital money serves as an important solution. According to the World Bank's 2017 data, approximately 1.7 billion adults worldwide do not have a bank account (Demirgüç-Kunt et al. 2018). At this point, it is seen how digital financial tools facilitate participation in economic activities by overcoming the limitations of the traditional banking system.

As mentioned before, the M-Pesa application serves as a convincing model for advancing financial inclusion, acting as an affordable and accessible mobile payment platform that allows users to transfer dollars, make payments, and save money without requiring a bank account. The Kenyan economy has grown significantly through this platform and has been financed by over

50 million people (Mbiti & Weil 2016). M-Pesa is also known to increase the economic independence of rural women by promoting gender equality (Suri & Jack 2016).

It is known that financial inclusion deeply affects both individual and societal dimensions, and digital financial tools increase the sustainability of local economies by strengthening economic resilience during crises. During the COVID-19 pandemic, digital payment technology has made important financial transactions possible for people who do not have access to traditional banking systems (World Bank 2021).

Assistance for Small and Medium Enterprises

Small- and medium-sized firms are essential for economic growth and job creation. The difficulties small businesses face in obtaining funding represent a significant obstacle to their growth. Digital finance functions as an essential tool in overcoming these obstacles. Digital payment systems like Stripe and PayPal have expedited the incorporation of SMEs into the digital economy by facilitating swift and cost-effective payment processing (Chen & Zhang 2020).

A significant advantage of digital finance for SMEs is that it is faster and easier than traditional credit methods. SMEs can obtain basic cash using P2P lending platforms. Thanks to these platforms, companies can quickly obtain loans, bypassing the cumbersome processes of traditional banks (Gomber et al. 2018). Finance Circle in the US speeds up the financial transactions of small- and medium-sized businesses by an average of 40 % (King 2018). In addition, digital financial instruments facilitate access to international markets for small- and medium-sized businesses. Companies can reach a worldwide customer base, thanks to digital payment and e-commerce platforms. Stripe facilitates international payment transactions for companies. SMEs can therefore increase their sales and maximize their operational efficiency (Schueffel 2016).

As a result, technologies such as AI and big data analytics allow SMEs to better understand their marketing plans and better understand customer behavior. These innovations provide small- and medium-sized businesses with a competitive advantage. Big data analytics can be used to more effectively manage target demographics and customize marketing plans (Wang & Yu 2021).

Challenges and Risks of Digital Finance: Regulation, Security, and Societal Impacts

Digital finance has many advantages that support economic growth and social progress, but it also presents some problems and dangers. This section will discuss the legal issues of digital currency, cybersecurity dangers, and economic inequality.

Regulatory Concerns

The rapid proliferation of digital financial instruments has brought with it problems in complying with legal regulations. Conventional financial systems have functioned within a specific regulatory framework for numerous years. Nevertheless, the characteristics of digital money may render creative company models beyond the purview of current regulatory restrictions. Blockchain technology and decentralized financial (DeFi) applications specifically encounter regulatory ambiguities (Arner et al. 2015). Regulations like the European Union's PSD2 have facilitated open banking and heightened competition between FinTech startups and banks. However, these limitations are far from being a global standard. Digital finance is becoming more difficult to use internationally due to different regulatory frameworks of major economies such as the US, China, and Europe. This poses a significant obstacle to the integration of digital financial services worldwide (Demirgüç-Kunt et al. 2018). Regulatory issues are apparent at both international and local levels. In undeveloped nations, insufficient regulatory frameworks might hinder the expansion and acceptance of digital finance. Governments must formulate equitable rules that safeguard consumer rights and maintain market stability while promoting innovation (Schueffel 2016).

Cybersecurity Vulnerabilities

Cybersecurity threats are very dangerous for digital money. Financial institutions are becoming more vulnerable to cybercriminals with the increasing digitalization. The security of digital financial systems is especially at great risk from major data breaches, fraud, and ransomware (Wang & Yu 2021). Digital payment systems and blockchain platforms utilize advanced encryption technologies to mitigate security issues. Nonetheless, these technologies may not consistently ensure adequate security. The $600 million hacking attack on a DeFi platform in 2021 underscored the security issues inherent in decentralized financial systems (Chen & Zhang 2020). To mitigate the effects of cybersecurity risks, both the commercial and public sectors must implement appropriate measures. Big data analytics and AI-driven monitoring systems can avert possible dangers by identifying anomalous activities promptly. Furthermore, it is imperative for governments and regulatory authorities to establish cybersecurity standards and guarantee adherence by all market participants (Gomber et al. 2018).

Income Inequality

When digital banking is not accessible, social inequalities can increase. Digital financial services typically require internet connectivity, digital capabilities, and mobile devices. Those with limited financial resources or living in rural areas may be at risk of these restrictions (Mbiti & Weil 2016). The digital divide has the potential to exacerbate income inequality. In developing countries, the limited accessibility of FinTech to a select few hinders the full realization of the digital economy's benefits. Research indicates that the absence of suitable targeting and instructional initiatives in digital financial services can exacerbate social inequalities (Suri & Jack 2016). Governments ought to establish initiatives aimed at improving access to digital financial tools and advancing digital literacy. Moreover, the cost-effectiveness of mobile financial services would enhance accessibility for a wider audience. The Jan Dhan Yojana effort in India shows efficient financial inclusion by providing free bank accounts to low-income individuals (World Bank 2021).

Conclusion: The Transformation Power of Digital Finance and Future Perspectives

Digital finance disrupts the global economy by expanding financial systems. The advanced technology of digital finance offers new options for individuals, companies, and communities by providing fast, easy, and effective services. The important role of digital finance in reducing economic and social inequalities is highlighted by the progress in financial inclusion and the inclusion of SMEs in the digital economy. However, digital finance has its advantages and disadvantages. Lack of regulation prevents new business models from complying with legal regulations, while cybersecurity issues threaten the security of digital financial systems. An important social dimension of this transformation process is income inequality, which is caused by the lack of access to digital financial services for all individuals.

In the future, technologies such as AI, blockchain, and big data analytics are expected to significantly affect the development of digital banking. AI improves the automation of financial processes and reduces costs, while blockchain technology promotes the security and transparency of transactions. The privatization of financial services will grow with big data analytics. Blockchain-based digital currencies are expected to reduce the cost of international trade and increase the integration of financial systems. Therefore, digital money serves as a revolutionary tool to increase social justice and promote economic growth. To fulfill this promise, it is necessary to improve laws, reduce cybersecurity issues, and close digital gaps. In the future, digital finance will play a significant role in advancing a more equitable and sustainable global economy with the help of technology.

CHAPTER 2

Green Finance Revolution: Pioneering Sustainability and Sustainable Investment for a Better Tomorrow

Serkan Yeşilyurt

ABSTRACT
In recent years, the increasing demands of human consumption and the rapid growth of the global population have led to significant environmental degradation. This chapter provides an in-depth exploration of sustainable finance, a critical response to these challenges. Sustainable finance refers to the integration of environmental, social, and governance (ESG) criteria into financial services to promote long-term environmental sustainability and social responsibility. The necessity for sustainable finance arises from the urgent need to mitigate the adverse effects of human activities on the environment and to ensure a sustainable future for future generations. This study begins with an introduction to sustainable finance, outlining the factors that have driven its emergence. It highlights the escalating consumption patterns and the consequent environmental damage, emphasizing the pressing need for sustainable financial practices. The definition and management of sustainable finance are discussed, elucidating why it has become an essential component of modern financial systems. The core of the study delves into the various instruments of sustainable finance, categorized into sustainable green debt instruments and sustainable credits. Green debt instruments include Green Bonds, Green Asset-Backed Securities (Green ABSs), Sustainable Bonds, Social Bonds, Green Municipal Bonds, and Sustainability-Linked Bonds (SLBs). On the other hand, sustainable credits encompass Green Loans, Social Loans, and Sustainability-Linked Loans (SLLs). I try to examine how these instruments function and their role in promoting environmental sustainability. Furthermore, this study discusses the growing appetite of investors for sustainable investments, driven by a sense of responsibility toward environmental conservation. It explores global trends in sustainable finance, such as ESG investments, the circular economy, green bonds, social bonds, and carbon bonds. These trends reflect a shift toward more sustainable financial practices worldwide. There is a critical role of sustainable finance in addressing global environmental challenges and fostering a more sustainable and equitable future.

Keywords: Sustainable finance, ESG, climate change, Green finance, Green Bonds

Jel Codes: Z23, Q56

Introduction

The effects of the current financial system on the environment and climate, and the negative impact of deepening climate change on economic activities, have led to accelerated efforts on a global scale to make financial sectors more sustainable, especially after the Paris Climate Agreement (EU Green Deal). The damage caused to nature by human beings through intensive mechanization has reached high levels over the years. Concepts such as resource nationalism, circular economy, and sustainable life have also become conceptualized over time and started to appear increasingly. The Paris Climate Agreement, which entered into force in 2016, includes various measures to mitigate the adverse effects of climate change and adapt to climate change process, as well as various provisions on climate finance. In the final declaration published after the United Nations (UN) 27th Conference of the Parties held in November 2022, it is estimated that an investment of at least $4–6 trillion per year is needed in the transition to a low-carbon economy by 2030 in order to achieve the 2050 global net emission target (Şimşek et al. 2024). Although green transformation is very costly, the majority of the financing for ensuring this transformation worldwide is met by public resources. One of the commitments of the Paris Agreement is the failure to fulfill the annual financing of $100 billion that should be provided from developed countries to developing countries to ensure green transformation, which shows that there is a serious resource requirement here. In addition to public resources, channeling private sector resources as a complement to the transition to a climate-neutral, climate-resilient, and fair economy is of great importance in the fight against climate change (Şimşek et al. 2024). Banks and other financial institutions play a major role in the realization of green transformation projects. They indirectly, if not directly, support companies' sustainability efforts or endeavors through sustainability-related loans and Green Loan options. These loans offer a broad perspective on issues such as carbon neutral production or renewable energy investments of companies, efforts to reduce carbon emissions, increasing women's employment, etc. The financing provided for the realization of climate-oriented objectives is divided into two as "sustainable financing" and "green financing." While the term sustainable refers to ESG, which is an umbrella concept, the term green refers to environmental issues.

The concept of sustainability was introduced to the literature in 1987 with the "Our Common Future" report of the UN World Commission on Environment and Development. There is no single universally accepted definition of sustainability. However, it is mostly defined as *meeting today's needs without compromising the ability of future generations to meet their own needs.* It means being both socially and ecologically permanent while ensuring the continuity of production, diversity, and consumption. While talking about what sustainability is, we should also look at it from the other side. *So what is not sustainability?* The most common misconception is to limit sustainability only to ecology. However, sustainability is a holistic approach that recognizes that everything should be considered together to establish lasting prosperity. If we continue with the question of what sustainability covers. At the 2005 World Summit on Social Development, it was stated that the three dimensions of sustainability are not mutually independent and may even be mutually binding, and the system was expressed with a picture using three intertwined ellipses.

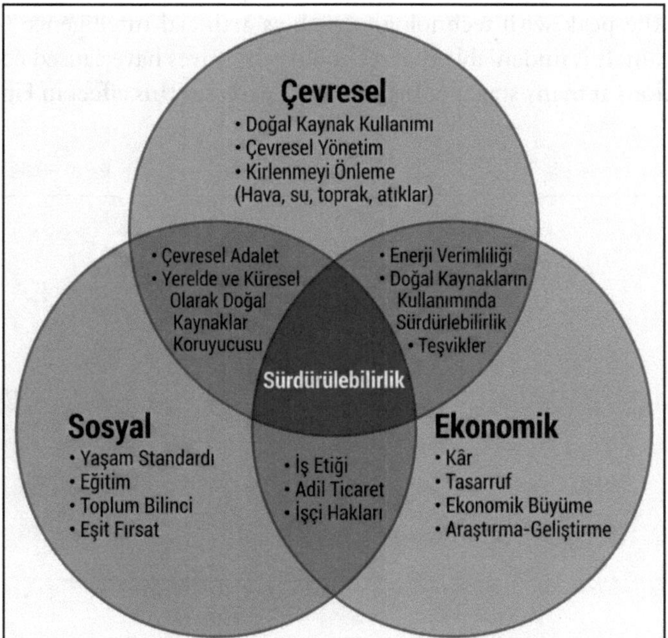

Figure 2.1. Sustainable theme.
Source: sepa.org.tr

Sustainability has different dimensions: economy, society, and environment. In other words, adopting a lifestyle that respects the environment is not synonymous with sustainability. It requires adding factors such as social equality, economic development, and welfare to the equation and taking steps to ensure that all human activities exist in balance.

How Did We Get Here Today?

In the history of technology, it is seen that technological innovations lead to economic waves. For example, the wave that started with the introduction of steam technology in the 1845s and subsequent technological innovations in the railway industry, the second wave that started with innovations such as electricity and internal combustion engines in the 1900s, followed by electrical technology and computer technology, and nowadays, it is running toward the peak with technologies such as artificial intelligence (AI) and blockchain. It is undeniable that technological waves have caused economic fluctuations at many stages of history. We clearly see this effect in Figure 2.2.

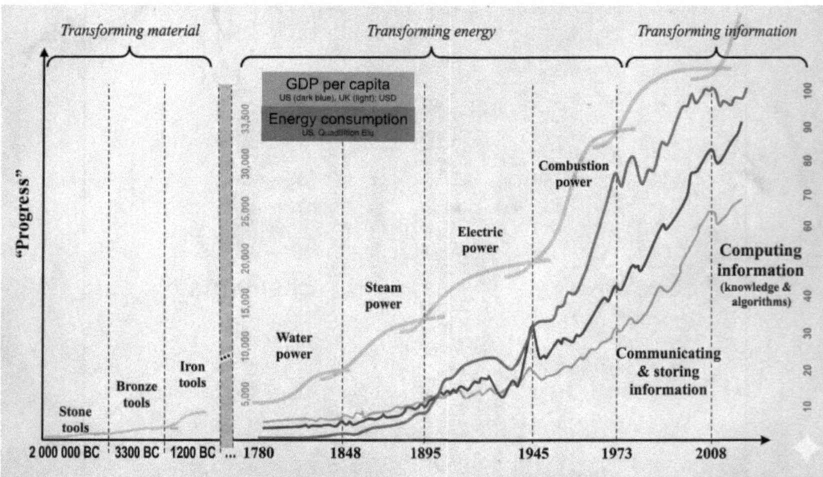

Figure 2.2. Schematic representation of Schumpeterian long waves. GDP, gross domestic product (Hilbert 2020).
Source: (Blok 2023)

Technological developments also bring a new world order. The development of steam technology and the development of the order road supported rapid transportation from rural areas to city centers, and people started to try their luck there. In addition, with the industrial revolution and steam technology, we see that large amounts of raw materials are transported to city centers for processing, and a new socioeconomic order has emerged in these places. The science of economics, which arose from unlimited human needs and the necessity of managing them, began to search for a balance in this new order. Increasing human needs and how they can be met. While meeting these needs, we have come to the problem of whether we borrow from the future and continue our production today. This has brought us the phenomenon of sustainable production, one of the most important problems of today: To be able to produce and live in peace with nature, without disturbing nature and the natural balance. When we look at the rapidly increasing world population, the balance between technological development and production will be better understood.

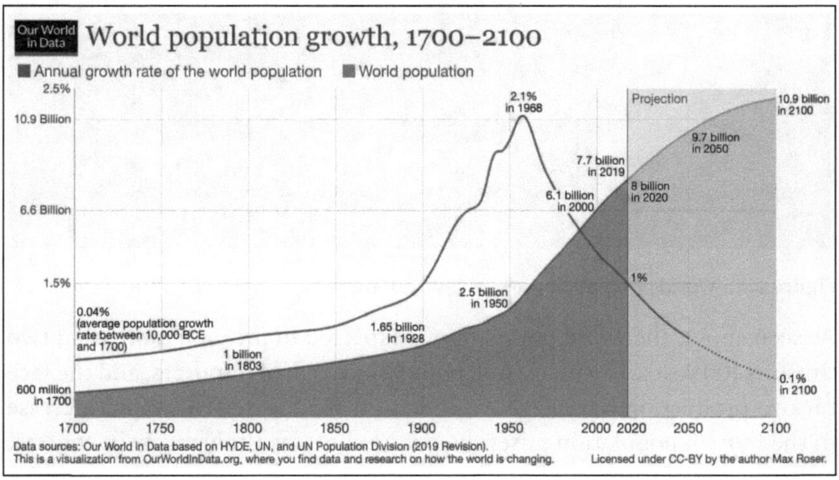

Figure 2.3. World population growth, 1700–2100.

Source: https://www.researchgate.net/figure/World-population-growth-1700-2100-Courtesy-https-ourworldindataorg-Urban_fig1_346651495

As human needs increase, technology has had to develop and evolve in order to respond to these increasing needs. The problem here is whether the developing technology has contributed to the multiplication of production while considering the environment. Today, when we look at all sectors, they plan their production in line with global trends, not counting the COVID-19 period. Today, although there is an inflation rate that has returned from very high levels, there is still an inflation rate and fear of inflation that continues to hover at high levels. So why do we need sustainable finance? What is the role of sustainable finance between production on one side and consumption on the other? How will it support sustainability? Before answering these questions, we should first refer to the Sustainable Development Goals (SDGs).

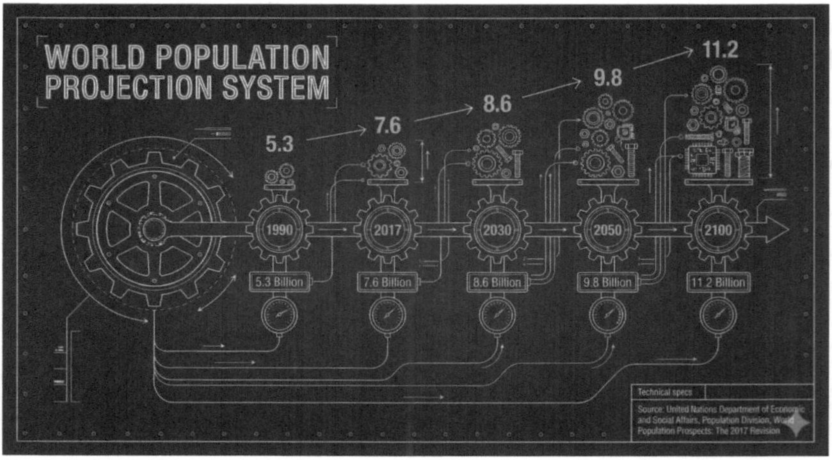

Figure 2.4. World population growth, 1990–2100.

As seen above, the world population is expected to increase more than two times in 100 years. The increasing population, lack of resources, and the race for overproduction have negative effects on the future. This rapid increase in the human population raises the question of unsustainability in contrast to the theme of sustainability.

Sustainable Development Goals (SDGs)

The SDGs consist of 17 targets set within the framework of the 2030 Agenda for Sustainable Development, adopted by the UN in 2015. These goals cover a wide range from poverty eradication to environmental sustainability. Here are the 17 SDGs:

Figure 2.5. UN SDGs.

These 17 goals provide a comprehensive roadmap for development, environmental protection, and social equity around the world. Each goal is critical for a sustainable future, primarily by bringing together social, economic, and environmental dimensions. One of the pillars of sustainable development is the sustainable economy, circular economy, and therefore, the effective utilization of financial resources. To consolidate the theme of sustainability, many international institutions and organizations are working to internalize the issue. In this sense, many agreements have been put into force and are being tried to be put into force.

Basic Concepts in Sustainable Finance

Sustainable finance is an approach that considers the economic, social, and environmental impacts of financial activities. This approach focuses on financial decisions not only on short-term gains but also on long-term sustainability and social benefits (Istanbul Chamber of Industry Sustainability Report 2014).[1] In this direction, the basic concepts that should be known about the subject are as follows:

ESG Criteria: These criteria, which include ESG factors, evaluate the sustainability performance of companies and investments.

Green Financing: A type of financing directed toward environmental projects, renewable energy investments, or energy efficiency projects.

---

1 Istanbul Chamber of Industry Sustainability Report 2014, https://www.iso.org.tr/corporate/ici-sustainability-reports/. (The report has been removed from the website.)

Social Investment: These are investments made for social benefit. These investments focus on objectives such as ensuring social justice and increasing social welfare.

Ethical Investment: Making investment decisions according to ethical values and social responsibility principles.

Microfinance: A type of financing that provides financial services for low-income individuals or small businesses.

Carbon Mitigation: Financial instruments that aim to reduce *carbon* emissions.

Social Responsibility: Social responsibility in finance involves considering the social impact of investments and financial activities. This may include investing in businesses that promote fair labor practices, community development, and access to essential services such as healthcare and education. Socially responsible investing often involves eliminating investments in industries such as tobacco or firearms.

Literature Review

Previous literature reviews on sustainable finance were summarized in Table 2.1.

Table 2.1. Literature review.

Authors	Title	Purpose of Study	Year	Journal / Source	Main Findings
Rezende et al.	A systematic review of the literature on finance and sustainability.	To review literature based on finance and sustainability, and highlight gaps in articles published in the Journal of Sustainable Finance & Investment	2016	Journal of Sustainable Finance & Investment	It is essential to concentrate on finance, investment, and sustainability in developing nations, the formulation of a conceptual standard, methods for assessing impact in social and organizational contexts, and the involvement of public and private sector banks in sustainability initiatives.

(Continued)

Table 2.1. *Continued*

Authors	Title	Purpose of Study	Year	Journal / Source	Main Findings
Kraus et al.	Sustainable entrepreneurship orientation: A reflection on status quo research on factors facilitating responsible managerial practices.	To understand the sustainable financial markets for entrepreneurs	2018	Sustainability	Require an analysis of the correlation between ethical practices and business financial performance, as well as an examination of the role of entrepreneurs in facilitating social change, among other factors.
Martínez-Climent et al.	Sustainable financing through crowdfunding.	To study how crowdfunding and sustainable orientation of crowdfunded ventures were related	2019	Sustainability	Emphasized the necessity for increased contributions to sustainable environmental and social initiatives for crowdfunded businesses.
Linnenluecke et al.	Sixty years of accounting and finance: A bibliometric analysis of major research themes and contributions.	To analyze all articles in the last 60 years in Accounting & Finance and incorporate economic, environmental, and social topics	2020	Accounting and Finance	Focus on integrated reporting, FinTech and environmental research, sustainable finance, the impact of climate change on corporate revenues and assets, and climate-related risks. COVID-19 and sustainability.
Cunha et al.	Sustainable finance and investment: Review and research agenda.	To map the sustainable finance and investment area with upcoming research avenues	2021	Business Strategy and the Environment	The research proposed a framework of options for sustainable financing and investment. It also suggested various research questions and their approaches.
Luo et al.	Global evolution of research on sustainable finance from	To map the evolution of sustainable finance	2022	Sustainability	Future themes in the green bonds market include ESG green finance (such as

(*Continued*)

Table 2.1. *Continued*

Authors	Title	Purpose of Study	Year	Journal / Source	Main Findings
	2000 to 2021: A bibliometric analysis on the WoS database.				SRI funds and ESG ratings), corporate-level green finance (including social capital in environmental projects), and green recovery post-COVID-19.
Kumar et al.	Past, present, and future of sustainable finance: Insights from big data analytics through machine learning of scholarly research.	To provide a wide spectrum review of sustainable finance and map its evolution	2022	Annals of Operations Research	Propose research inquiries pertaining to the application of technology in sustainable finance, the development of innovative financial instruments, the enhancement of investment returns via sustainable investments, the formulation of new laws and frameworks, and the influence of behavioral finance on sustainable finance.
Tao et al.	Environmental finance: An interdisciplinary review.	To provide a systematic review of papers in environmental finance from a financial perspective	2022	Technological Forecasting and Social Change	Proposed study subjects include climate finance, sustainable finance, the influence of non-financial disclosures on firm valuation, climate risk, and green bonds.
Canikli	Sustainable finance mechanisms and the sustainable development relationship.	To show the relationship between the financial mechanism and the sustainable economy	2022	Akdeniz İİBF Journal	This paper examines the function of sustainable finance in funding investments for sustainable development and climate change mitigation. It underscores the significance of tackling environmental, socioeconomic,

(*Continued*)

Table 2.1. *Continued*

Authors	Title	Purpose of Study	Year	Journal / Source	Main Findings
					and governance concerns. The paper assesses the influence of the COVID-19 epidemic on sustainable finance and related domains, highlighting its significance in attaining sustainable development objectives.
Ren et al.	Sustainable finance and blockchain: A systematic review and research agenda.	To perform a systematic analysis of blockchain in renewable, sustainable finance	2023	Research in International Business and Finance	Factors concerning sustainable financial application development utilizing blockchain and other technological innovations, emerging social challenges with financial dangers, and identified concerns associated with AI and cryptocurrency.
Şimşek et al.	Cyclical analysis of sustainable and green financial instruments.	To assess the effect of investment decisions on the environment	2024	Balkan Journal of Social Sciences	This study examines sustainable finance in developing countries and Turkey, examining its current state, technical characteristics, and use. It also discusses obstacles and constraints to sustainable financing, and suggests suggestions for developing sustainable capital market debt instruments in Turkey. The goal is to increase long-term investment in sustainable economic activities.

(*Continued*)

Table 2.1. *Continued*

Authors	Title	Purpose of Study	Year	Journal / Source	Main Findings
Khamitdkhanovich et al.	Green finance and ESG investing: Driving sustainable growth through innovation.	The purpose of the study is to assess how green finance and ESG investment support sustainable development, what obstacles they face, and how innovations and regulations can enhance their effectiveness in fostering a low-carbon, resilient global economy.	2025	AIP Publishing/ Conference Proceedings	The study finds that while green finance and ESG investing are reshaping global finance toward sustainability, their full potential depends on stronger regulation, consistent measurement standards, and the integration of emerging technologies to ensure credibility and long-term impact.

Defining Sustainable Finance

Sustainability is one of the most talked-about topics today. We can even use this adjective in front of everything. For example,

- **sustainable environment;**
- **sustainable living;**
- **sustainable food;**
- **sustainable business life** … etc.

Of course, sustainable finance is one of these descriptions. The poem expressed by the Indian Chief Seattle in 1853, which many of us know, read in books, magazines, or come across in social media, expresses the situation we are in very clearly for many of us: "*When the last river runs dry, when the last tree dies, when the last fish dies, the white man will realise that money is inedible.*" The first sentence of Grand Chief Seattle's famous poem is the beginning of this sustainable finance endeavor:

"The white man looks upon the earth, his mother, and the sky, his sister, as something to be bought and sold, something to be plundered." This statement shows how wrong it is and how appropriate these sustainable finance discussions are.

When we ask what the purpose of a business is, we get the answer "to maximise the profits of the business." Even in the 1970s, Milton Friedman *argued that "the only social responsibility of business is profit maximisation. Any favour to customers or employees doing the work is incidental. If maximising profits meant laying off employees and giving poor service to customers, that was fine with Friedman."* I wonder if Friedman is still right today. Of course, in today's world, Friedman's idea is not as valid as it was in the 1970s. Today, we can easily say that Friedman was wrong. Financial institutions can directly and indirectly cause serious damage to the environment. Human beings, who have been responsible for the damage to nature for centuries, need to eliminate this damage through various practices and regulations. It is also known how effective various financial practices implemented with the aim of reducing environmental damages can be in reducing these damages (Canikli 2022).

Sustainable finance is an approach that aims to create long-term value by taking into account the environmental and social impacts of financial decisions. This approach is a tool for dealing with global challenges:

- *climate change*,
- *natural resource scarcity*, and
- *social inequality*.

ESG criteria, which are the basic elements of sustainable finance, are used to evaluate the ESG performance of companies and investments. Investors tend to evaluate companies according to ESG criteria and invest in line with sustainability goals. ESG criteria can be explained as follows:

1) **Environmental Factors:** *Sustainable finance evaluates the positive and negative impacts on the environment. In particular, environmental issues such as climate change, energy efficiency, and protection of water resources have an impact on financial decisions. Areas such as green energy investments,*

waste management, water saving, and environmentally friendly production processes are part of sustainable finance.

2) **Social Factors:** *Social sustainability aims to improve the welfare of society and ensure social justice. Sustainable finance focuses on social issues such as education, health, employment, and income justice. Social investments and social enterprises play an important role in this area.*
3) **Governance:** *Governance processes of companies are important for the effective implementation of sustainable finance. Transparency, accountability, and interaction with stakeholders are important elements of good governance.*

Source: *Istanbul Chamber of Industry Sustainability Report, March 2024*

(https://www.iso.org.tr/corporate/ici-sustainability-reports/. The report has been removed from the website.)

We can say that the meaning ascribed to it definitionally has evolved and changed over time. For example, looking back to the early days of the rise of the ESG concept in general, sustainable finance largely meant that the financial system should incorporate sustainability considerations into investment decision-making to better reflect environmental and other sustainability-related risks. With the evolution in societal and policy patterns, the meaning of sustainable finance is increasingly consolidated around the need to provide sufficient financial resources for the transition to a more sustainable society and a climate-neutral economy. This change in perspective may help to explain the recent acceleration in the adoption of sustainable finance practices by financial institutions (Arslan 2022).

Sustainable finance is a concept related to the domestic or global financing of investments that support SDGs and aim to mitigate or adapt to climate change. Contrary to the risk and return concepts of traditional finance, the aim of sustainable finance is to provide resources for investments that stand out in ESG areas (Canikli 2022). There are different types of sustainable finance, which are shown in Table 2.2.

Why Is Sustainable Finance Needed?

Today's economic model is largely based on a linear structure and ignores environmental risks. This puts serious pressure on economic resources. With population growth and changing consumer behavior, annual resource

Table 2.2. Types of sustainable finance.

Typology	Author	Concept
Environmental finance	Linnenluecke et al. (2016)	The connections between the planetary boundaries and the influence of environmental concerns on financial decision-making were discussed in environmental finance. Green finance and carbon were covered.
Green Finance	IFC (2017)	It targeted financial activities that diminished pollutants and greenhouse gas emissions, offered other environmental advantages, and facilitated economic growth.
Social finance	Geobey et al. (2012); Rizzi et al. (2018)	It sought to address social issues through social innovations, microfinance, social banking, and impact investing.
Carbon finance	Lewis (2010); Mohsin et al. (2020)	It encompassed all financial strategies to mitigate greenhouse gas emissions, including carbon credits, emissions trading, and the clean development mechanism.
Climate finance	Zadek (2011); Hong et al. (2020)	It sought to fund climate mitigation and adaptation initiatives by utilizing both private and governmental financing. It is a component of green financing.
SDG Finance	Migliorelli (2021)	It sought to advance inclusive financing through the enhancement of financial innovation and the digitization of sustainable strategies and investments. It also aimed to enhance the influence of ESG on the economy, society, and the environment through various financial instruments.

Source: *Singhania et al. 2023*

consumption has increased from 7 billion tons in the early 1900s to more than 60 billion tons in 2005. In 2050, this figure is expected to reach 140 million tons. The problems that current resource consumption trends may create are quite worrying. Existing resource consumption causes many problems. These are as follows in order:

- The problem of resource scarcity in the future is a result of the rapid consumption of resources.
- Increasing greenhouse gases and waste is a major environmental problem in the future.

- Lack of access to economic resources for future generations.
- Deterioration of soil quality for healthy agriculture.
- The rapid increase in inflation and the danger of chronicity for the whole world.
- Problems of clean air and water supply.
- Decreasing biodiversity and increasing danger of extinction of some species.

Global Sustainable Finance

The ability or capacity of each country or organization to combat climate change varies. Sustainable finance has a key role in fulfilling the commitments regarding climate and sustainability targets under the Paris Climate Agreement, which aims to combat climate change (Şimşek et al. 2024). The emergence of sustainable financial instruments *(Green Bonds, Sustainable Bonds, Green Municipal Bonds, Green Municipal Bonds, Green Loans, Green Securitization, Social Bonds, SLBs, and SLLs)* and the financing of activities whose issuance meets certain criteria have created an awareness and sensitivity on this issue in the real sector. The fact that the private sector is a part of these efforts, the impact of which will be seen in the long term and strengthens the reputation of the company, and the feeling of contributing to the future of the world, positively affects the interest of companies in green financial instruments. Sustainable financial instruments can be categorized into two categories:

(i) sustainable green debt instruments;
(ii) sustainable loan.

Sustainable Finance Investment Instruments and Their Impact

Sustainable Green Debt Instruments

Green Bonds: Green bonds are bonds issued to support the financing of sustainable projects. These bonds are particularly used to finance projects that provide environmental benefits. Green bonds are used to finance environmental projects such as clean energy, energy efficiency, and environmentally friendly infrastructure. Green bonds were first issued in Scotland in 2007. Green bonds have become increasingly popular in recent years, and the total market value of green bonds issued in 2024 exceeded US $1 trillion (Climate Bonds Report).

Green ABSs: Green ABSs are financial instruments issued to achieve environmental sustainability goals. These securities are generally used to finance environmental projects such as renewable energy projects, energy efficiency, clean transport, and sustainable water management.

Sustainable Bonds: Sustainable bonds are financial instruments issued to achieve both environmental and social sustainability goals. These bonds offer the flexibility to invest in a wider range of projects and activities than green bonds. They are used to finance environmentally friendly projects, social development-themed projects, and sustainable transport-themed projects.

Social Bonds: These are financial instruments issued to provide social benefits. These bonds aim to support social development by financing social projects.

Green Municipal Bonds: These are financial instruments issued by municipalities to finance environmental sustainability projects. These bonds enable local governments to realize environmentally friendly projects.

SLBs: Financial instruments that incentivize the issuer to achieve specific sustainability goals. These bonds offer financial incentives based on the ESG performance of the issuer.

Sustainable Loans

Sustainability loans are basically loan products that take into account ESG factors. Sustainability loans aim to finance investments based on the idea of a sustainable economic structure. In this way, it is aimed to provide an advantageous financial environment for projects with a lower carbon footprint, high social contribution, longer-term profit, and social benefit (ING Sustainability Report).

Green Loans: These are financial instruments issued to achieve environmental sustainability goals. These loans support sustainable development by financing environmental projects.

Social Loans: These are used to finance projects with a social impact. Projects that aim to contribute to areas with high social impact, such as

Table 2.3. Sustainable finance products by product type and market.

$ billion					
	Mature markets	*Emerging markets*	*Offshore centers*	*Supranationals*	*Global*
Sustainable debt securities	**$ 3.408,22**	**$ 750,22**	**$ 74,46**	**$ 834,75**	**$ 5.067,65**
Green bonds	$ 1.926,63	$ 451,31	$ 61,37	$ 202,77	$ 2.642,08
Green ABS	$ 258,31	$ 14,22	$ -	$ -	$ 272,53
	$ 362,64	$ 163,13	$ 2,63	$ 464,37	$ 992,78
Sustainability bonds	$ 511,19	$ 55,06	$ 7,61	$ 167,51	$ 741,37
Social bonds	$ 148,92	$ -	$ -	$ -	$ 148,92
Green muni bonds	$ 200,54	$ 66,49	$ 2,84	$ 0,10	$ 269,97
Sustainable loans	**$ 1.501,15**	**$ 339,17**	**$ 145,62**	**$ 0,03**	**$ 1.986,00**
Green loans	$ 494,56	$ 207,12	$ 63,34	$ 0,06	$ 765,07
Sustainability-linked loans	$ 1.006,60	$ 132,05	$ 82,28	$ -	$ 1.220,93
Total	**$ 4.909,37**	**$ 1.089,40**	**$ 220,08**	**$ 834,78**	**$ 7.053,65**

Source: IIE 2024, as of October.

education, housing, health, unemployment, or social rehabilitation, are financed with this product.

SLLs: These are financial instruments that incentivize the issuer to achieve certain sustainability goals. These loans offer financial incentives based on the issuer's ESG performance.

Table 2.3 and Figure 2.6 show the extent of sustainable finance investments and expectations for 2024. Increasing the utilization of this product range in emerging markets constitutes one of the important agenda items.

Also, Figure 2.6 is a chart with the issuance of global sustainability-linked financial instruments.

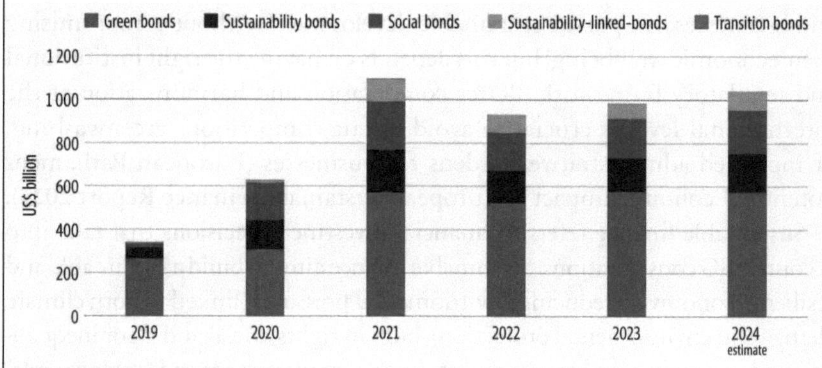

Data source: EPRS using Standard and Poor.

Figure 2.6. Global sustainability financial instrument issuances ($ billion).

There is a global trend, particularly in Europe, in the issuance of sustainability-themed instruments, which is influenced by the desire both to finance environmental projects and to invest in companies with high environmental sensitivity from an investor perspective.

Impacts of Sustainable Lending

Sustainable finance refers to the process of taking ESG considerations into account when making investment decisions in the financial sector. This can lead investors to invest more in the transition toward a climate-neutral, climate-resilient, resource-efficient, and equitable economy with a high level of quality governance requirements. Sustainable finance, therefore, has a key role to play in realizing the policy objectives under the European Green Deal. In this regard, the EU has made significant progress in recent years, notably with the adoption of the sustainable finance action plan in 2018, the renewed strategy for financing the transition to a sustainable economy in 2021, and several legislative proposals. As a result, the EU is well-positioned in this area with an estimated €6.6 trillion of ESG assets under management in 2024, representing 38 % of total assets under management in the EU (€17.2 trillion). However, the relationship between sustainability efforts and a country's economic growth and its impact on business and financial performance remains a matter of debate. Recent research shows that countries and businesses can pursue sustainable development without compromising their economic well-being, but this depends on having the right institutional and regulatory framework. Better co-operation and harmonization at the international level is crucial to avoid unfair competition, greenwashing, or increased administrative burdens for businesses (European Parliament Potential Economic Impact of European Sustainable Finance Report 2024).

Sustainable finance refers to financial investment decisions that take into account ESG considerations. Sustainable finance aims to build a sustainable and resilient economy by reducing environmental pressures (linked to both climate change and environmental protection), human rights, social and labor inequalities, and improving governance aspects (such as management and employee relations), while strengthening long-term economic growth. Sustainable finance, therefore, also means increasing transparency of the risks associated with ESG factors that may affect the financial system and their mitigation.

Global sustainable investment assets are estimated at around €32.4 trillion in 2024 (European Parliament Potential Economic Impact of European Sustainable Finance Report 2024) and are projected to continue growing, reaching €40 trillion in 2030. The EU is well-positioned to benefit from this development as it currently has one of the highest amounts of sustainable assets under management, estimated at around €6.6 trillion in 2024, representing 38% of total assets under management in the EU (€17.2 trillion). This can be explained by the fact that the EU has been very active in establishing a regulatory framework to promote the development of sustainable finance.

The main environmental impacts of sustainability credits are as follows:

- **Reduction of Carbon Emissions:** Projects financed with sustainability credits contribute to the reduction of carbon emissions through less fossil fuel consumption.
- **Energy savings:** Financed projects lead to lower energy consumption through products and services that consume less energy.
- **Renewable Energy:** The energy-generating companies financed with this loan contribute to the development of renewable energy sources such as solar farms, wind power, bioenergy, and hydroelectric power plants. According to 2021 data, the share of renewable energy sources in

all energy production is 11 % globally. Some countries, such as Sweden and Denmark, have already started to meet all their electricity needs from renewable sources.
- **Water Saving:** Projects financed with these loans contribute to more efficient use of water resources.
- **Waste Management:** Projects that also provide services in areas such as recycling and biomass contribute to a sustainable future in the field of waste management.
- **Low-Carbon Economy:** This promotes investments that prioritize ESG issues through strategic allocation of capital. Among its critical components, green investments and energy transition stand out as key drivers. Green investments direct financial resources toward projects and initiatives with positive environmental impacts. This includes renewable energy projects, energy-efficient technologies, sustainable agriculture, and more. These investments reduce the carbon footprint and contribute to the development of a resilient and sustainable infrastructure. Simultaneously, the energy transition focuses on the shift from fossil fuels toward cleaner, renewable energy sources.

Global Trends and Regulations

Sustainable finance aims to support economic growth by taking into account ESG factors. The concept has evolved in response to global challenges such as climate change, natural resource depletion, and social inequalities. The rise of sustainable finance in the global context has led to radical changes in both economic and legal regulations. Important global trends include the European Green Deal, ESG investments, and carbon trading.

Increase in ESG Investments

ESG investments, which include ESG criteria, have gained an important place in financial markets. According to Bloomberg, the total size of ESG assets has exceeded $50 trillion as of 2023. This amount is expected to reach $55 trillion in 2025 (Bloomberg 2023). Investors prefer companies based on factors such as environmental sustainability, employee welfare, and management ethics, recognizing that long-term profitability depends on these factors.

While traditional finance focuses solely on financial risk and return, responsible or sustainable finance, on the contrary, is the key to moving from the narrow partnership model we know to a broader partnership model that takes into account the combination of financial, social, and environmental returns. Another important concept within the sustainable framework is the concept of responsible investment (Responsible Investment).

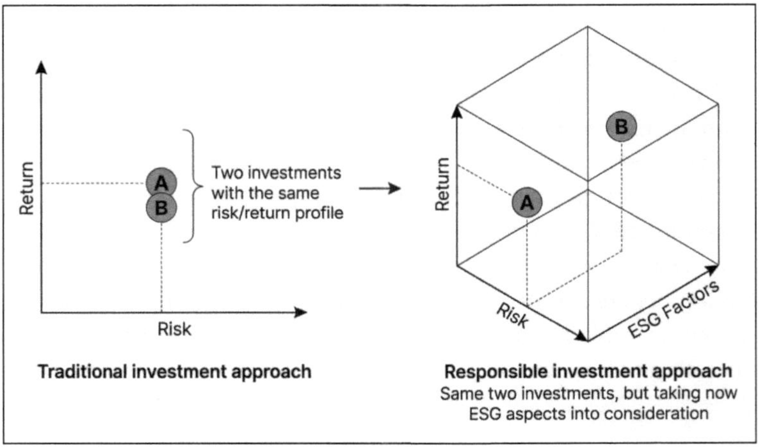

Figure 2.7. Traditional financial approach and responsible investment.

In the traditional investment approach, two investments are at the same risk-return level, whereas in responsible investment, that is, sustainable finance, two products are no longer at the same risk and return level.

In addition, investors also shape their investment preferences by considering the environmental sensitivity of companies. The existence of a sustainability index consisting of environmentally sensitive companies and the companies included in this index, and the fact that the environmental factor has become one of the main problems, increases sensitivity in this area, both in the public and private sectors.

Circular Economy Models

The circular economy is an important component of sustainable finance. This model aims to optimize the use of natural resources, increase recycling rates, and minimize waste. According to a report by the Ellen MacArthur Foundation, the circular economy approach has the potential to increase GDP in the European Union by 7 % (Ellen MacArthur Foundation 2020). In industries such as glass and chemicals, this model is critical for improving the efficiency of resource use and reducing carbon emissions.

Green Bonds and Social Bonds

One of the fastest-growing instruments in the sustainable finance market is green bonds. These bonds finance projects such as renewable energy, energy efficiency, and low-carbon technologies. In 2022, green bond issuances worldwide reached $1 trillion (Climate Bonds Initiative 2022). Social bonds are used to fund social projects and have played an important role in health and education projects, especially in the post-pandemic period.

Carbon Markets

Carbon markets are an important tool to reduce emissions and ensure that companies fulfill their environmental responsibilities. Carbon credits allow companies to offset their emissions (International Carbon Action Partnership).

Regulations

European Union Taxonomy of Sustainable Finance: The EU has developed a taxonomy to define sustainable economic activities. This taxonomy helps investors to identify and report on sustainable investments.

Terralex International ESG and Sustainable Finance Guide: This guide provides detailed information on key ESG regulations and trends worldwide. The guide addresses critical issues such as legal disclosure obligations and shareholder rights, and measures against greenwashing.

Global Reporting Initiative (GRI): GRI sets international standards for companies to report their sustainability performance. These standards enable companies to transparently report their environmental and social impacts.

These trends and regulations encourage the adoption and implementation of sustainable finance on a global scale. By following these trends and regulations, companies can achieve their sustainability goals and support their long-term success.

Conclusion

Sustainable finance is an increasingly important field that has emerged in response to today's economic, environmental, and social challenges. In this study, basic concepts such as the definition and historical development of sustainability, SDGs, and international agreements are discussed in detail. It is emphasized that sustainability should be addressed not only with its environmental but also with its social and economic dimensions.

The scope and definition of sustainable finance, basic concepts in this field, and why sustainable finance is needed are emphasized. Global sustainable finance, sustainable investment principles, and ESG criteria are the cornerstones of sustainable finance. In this context, sustainable investment instruments and their impact sizes are analyzed, and the effects of sustainable loans, global trends, and regulations are detailed.

Sustainable finance promotes the consideration of ESG criteria in making investment decisions. This not only ensures that environmental and social responsibilities are fulfilled but also contributes to improving long-term financial performance. Sustainable loans help companies to reduce their environmental and social impact, while at the same time increasing their financial sustainability.

Sustainable finance strategies not only fulfill environmental and social responsibilities but also improve long-term financial performance. The effective use of sustainable financing instruments increases the competitive advantage of companies and contributes to the achievement of SDGs.

In conclusion, sustainable finance plays a vital role in building a sustainable future for both companies and societies. Sustainable finance strategies support the long-term success of companies, while also contributing to the achievement of global sustainability goals. This study highlights the importance of sustainable finance and the positive impacts of practices in this area on companies and societies.

CHAPTER 3

Circular Economy as a Pillar of Sustainability: Glass Recycling

Çağlar Yurtseven & Didem Cicerali

ABSTRACT
Due to limited natural resources and the necessity of the continuity of the ecosystem, the "take-make-dispose" approach has become more questionable recently. The new economic model, the circular economy, quickly gained global importance. The main purpose of the circular economy is to optimize the production–consumption relationship. It aims to reduce environmental impacts, produce further value with secondary raw materials, increase economic prosperity, and deliver benefits to future generations.

In this analysis, we focus on the glass industry, which is a prime example of the circularity of the economy because of its fully recyclable nature. Glass that is introduced into the economy without becoming waste by reuse, refill, or reproduction through melting decreases the use of resources, minimizes the cost of landfilling, and prevents environmental and air pollution. Considering its intensive recycling, glass is an essential material to ensure sustainability.

Keywords: Circular economy, sustainability, recycling, glass industry

Jel Codes: Q01, Q32, Q34

Introduction

The increasing need for resources following the inevitable population growth makes the issue of scarce resource allocation more critical and essential. The distribution of resources, which is already a major problem, increases its threat as the pie of resources shrinks and the number of stakeholders increases dramatically. The restructuring of the global production–consumption processes is necessary because it has reached unsustainable conditions and creates a climate crisis with the intensification of resource consumption. As emphasized by Esposito et al. (2018) if the production scheme and consumption habits remain stable, the depletion of natural resources cannot be prevented, and two planets' worth of natural resources will be needed by 2030 (Esposito et al. 2018; Abbas & Halog 2021).

The importance of sustainability increased as the scale of the foreseen problems grew. The UN is the global pioneer in this regard with the Sustainable Development Goals (SDGs). With the SDG-12 (Responsible Consumption and Production), the UN suggested that it is essential to change the patterns of rapid consumption. In addition, resource depletion should be prevented for sustainable development. The obligation of global cooperation to ensure economic, social, and environmental balance is also underlined (Assembly General 2015; Meloni et al. 2018; Schandl et al. 2020).

In the context of limited natural resources and the continuity of the ecosystem, the process of departure from the "take-make-dispose" approach of the ineffective traditional linear economic model is inevitable. The primary reason for this departure to a new economic model is the ineffective usage of finite natural resources in the production process. The infinite need for resources that cannot be met due to the continuous increase in consumer demand, and the inability to prevent waste, are the other major reasons. Under these limitations, the main motivation in this transition is to produce long-lasting products with fewer natural resources. Emphasis was placed on reducing resource usage by recycling products prior to the disposal stage (Sreedevi & Salahudeen 2021).

The new economic model, the circular economy, is also known as the closed-loop economy. The first step necessary for making the production process sustainable and efficient in the circular economy is to extend the lifespan of existing products through recycling or reuse. The circular economy aims to recycle/reuse the products that become waste after the use of consumers and, if this is not possible, to use that waste material as an input in a different industry. Hence, it would be envisaged to ensure circularity in the economy and resource usage (Abbas & Halog 2021; Sreedevi & Salahudeen 2021). Although it will not be completed in the short term, the transition from the traditional "take-make-dispose" structure of the economies to the circularization would bring new technology innovation and the growth in employment in this field (Sreedevi & Salahudeen 2021).

The deep meaning and importance attributed to sustainability necessitate the integration of countries, industries, and companies into the circular economy. Therefore, inevitably, the recipe of the circular economy, which includes resource usage reduction, slowing production through reuse, waste utilization with recycling, minimizing environmental damage, and creating added value with innovation and employment, would become the new global order.

Linear to Circular Economy

The linear economy, which represents the type of production that has been used since the beginning of industrialization, focuses on meeting the consumer's demand at minimum cost. Although resource efficiency was emphasized for many years, the understanding of the negative impact of the product becoming waste in a very short time on resource efficiency was only started at the beginning of the twentieth century. The main reason for this enlightenment is that the "take-make-dispose" system cannot be sustained with limited natural resources.

Because labor prices were higher than the other inputs in the relevant period, the production process was primarily built on natural resources and energy usage. Although this did not pose a problem at first, it caused natural resource owners to diverge in income distribution until the twentieth century. However, some consequences of resource consumption reaching alarming levels could not remain hidden any longer. Ellen MacArthur Foundation (2013) accepted the increase in commodity prices, which had been on a decreasing trend since the beginning of industrialization, in 1999, as a milestone in this regard. The reason for this increasing trend was the unsustainable substitution of human capital, due to the relatively high price, with natural resources and energy. As a result of excessive use of natural resources and energy to meet market demands, prices began to increase and became very volatile (MacArthur 2013; Sariatli 2017; Sreedevi & Salahudeen 2021).

The unsustainable problems of the linear economy can be listed as follows:

- substituting human capital for natural resources and energy in production process;
- under-utilization of resources;
- ignoring the environmental effects while focusing on mass production;
- production that becomes waste soon after purchase;
- lack of waste management and utilization (Radhakrishnan 2021).

The inability of the linear economy to innovate in these regards revealed the need to change the production–consumption process. This change is inevitable, coupled with the increase in input costs, the difficulty in accessing resources—means a reduction of profit margins—and the global popularity of sustainability. The inefficiency and inadequacy of the linear economy created competition in ensuring sustainable production.

The circular economy that focuses on reuse, recycle, and reduction as its three important principles aims to prevent production–consumption habits from working against nature and people.

The Rising Pivot of Sustainability: Circular Economy

The main purpose of the circular economy, built on renewability, recyclability, and sustainability, is to optimize the production–consumption relationship within the requirements. Although environmental and economic concerns date back to the 1960s, the term circular economy was first introduced to the literature by Pearce and Turner (1989). Environmental economists Pearce and Turner emphasized the wastefulness of traditional production patterns. They claimed that as long as economic systems are not circularized, the negative effects of consumption culture cannot be eliminated, and the world would be consumed and turned into a waste bin over time. According to them, the only method of optimization of the system is to apply the holistic approach to the entire production–consumption cycle and to reconstruct it in this direction (Pearce & Turner 1989; Radhakrishnan 2021). The first deep-rooted report on circularity in the economy was written by the Ellen MacArthur Foundation. The report, published in 2013, was inspired by the desire to build a sustainable future and stated that if today's challenges are not taken seriously, tomorrow's challenges can be irreversible. In this regard, we suggest transforming all elements of the linear economy (take-make-dispose) and regenerating it in line with the principle of holism (MacArthur 2013).

Starting from the focus on waste and resource efficiency, the circular economy that has become a holistic economic system is enabled sustainable development and growth and freed from negativity through restructuring. Considering current conditions, the concepts of development and growth are completely working against humankind. Producers, who want to meet the demand and maximize the profit margins, turn a blind eye to the damage to the environment and offer an unlimited supply to consumers. The realization that what is consumed is the future has brought with it sudden transformation demands (Su et al. 2013).

This new system basically aims to eliminate the concept of "end of life" shortly after the purchase of the product. It focuses on keeping existing resources and materials in the economy as long as possible for sustainability. In this way, it aims to reduce environmental impacts, produce further value with secondary raw materials, increase economic prosperity, and deliver benefits to future generations (Kirchherr et al. 2017; European Parliament [EP] 2017).

The *9R*'s strategy developed in macro (countries, cities, and regions), meso (eco-industrial parks), and micro (products and consumers) levels in this concept can be detailed as follows:

(R0) Refuse, focuses on changing the consumption habits of individuals in the context of sustainability. It aims to reconsider the needs and decide to decrease the amount of product used before purchase.

(R1) Rethink, making the product more intensive by sharing or including a multi-function feature.

(R2) Reduce, implies the use of resources at the stage of product configuration. This is the phase in which the efficient use of resources in the definition of the circular economy emerges. It also induces innovation with an effort to develop new techniques that make it possible to produce with less waste of input.

(R3) Reuse, means that the product does not leave the economy at the end of its first cycle. It is the continuation of the use of the product, which still fulfills its main function, by another user or in another area.

(R4) Repair, reuse of the product, which has a malfunction after its first cycle, by reconditioning after its first cycle.

(R5) Refurbish, use of old product through restoring.

(R6) Remanufacture, the transformation of the product that cannot be renewed or regain its original functions into a new form, rather than becoming waste. At this stage, remanufacturing is carried out with minimum waste by using existing parts of the old product, and it is aimed at restoring the original functions.

(R7) Repurpose, the process of revealing a product with new functions by using the parts of the defective product.

(R8) Recycle, making it possible to produce a new product by using the components of the product that have become unusable, by means of disassembly,

cleaning, sorting, etc. Essentially, this stage prevents waste. Recycling ensures that the product remains in the economy. This is the costliest and most innovative stage among strategies.

(R9) Recover, separation of products that have expired and cannot be recycled into their materials and reintroduce these materials into the production process. At this stage, energy use is at the forefront in terms of separation (Dyer et al. 2021; Asante et al. 2022).

The economy would be completed its circularity when all *9R* strategies are implemented. These strategies are shaped to enable three main purposes. The first of these main purposes is sustainable resource management. Given that the need for development and growth cannot be stopped, it is essential to find a way to deal with them. Since it is not possible to replenish the natural resources found on the planet, the management of existing resources is vital. The danger of producing as if there is no future is still around. The second purpose is to shape the social behavior of individuals in line with sustainable resource management. When we consider the supply of a product that is induced by demand, it is obvious that consumers cannot be ignored regarding the circularity of the economy. It is necessary to establish social norms in societies in a way that ensures the circularity of the economy. Individuals should be willing to share, reuse, and bear the increased costs of recycling for durability. Also, they should assist in the collection and sorting of products that need to be recycled instead of being wasted (Asante et al. 2022).

Finally, business models should employ the new order. It is imperative that businesses invest in designing their products in a durable manner. To ensure product circularity, they should make long-term projections and collect and reutilize waste even after the product becomes waste at the end of the cycle. Therefore, it is obvious that innovation is ineluctable in terms of sustainability. It would become more difficult for businesses that stay away from innovation to exist in the market (Chobanova 2020).

As it is easily understood, there is a duty for each stakeholder to undertake the circularization of the economy. However, still the most important duty in this regard is left to the governments and supranational organizations. The reason is that it is more likely that businesses and individuals would be unwilling to accept the additional costs of recycling. It is essential in the transition phase of the economy that governments support and maybe order recycling with new policies and legislations. Incentives and subsidies should be given to businesses for sustainable production, and governments should ensure that barriers to transition are eliminated. Public or private authorities should support the innovation required for sustainable energy and production techniques and penalize the toxic production–consumption (Abbas & Halog 2021).

The UN has recognized the circular economy as the only sustainable economic model available. With the SDG-12 (Responsible Consumption and Production), the importance of natural resources and the obligation of global cooperation to ensure economic, social, and environmental balance are underlined. The goals of sustainable management and efficient usage of resources are planned to be completed by 2030. UN mentioned the sub-targets as: to reduce waste in the production–consumption processes, to minimize the effects of waste and chemicals on people and the environment, to raise awareness of individuals of this issue, and to support sustainable employment for sustainable development (UN 2018).

The circular economy should be supported globally at all levels (macro, meso, and micro). The innovation or regulation required is unlikely to be successful by a single organization, government, and business (Schandl et al. 2020). The burden that is shared by all stakeholders would provide different benefits. From the point of view of governments, the circular production system would reduce the dependence on raw materials. Reducing the damage to the environment and the new level of economic prosperity achieved through sustainable development would be a common output (European Parliament [EP] 2017; Sreedevi & Salahudeen 2021).

It is aimed at ensuring circularity and recycling in all sectors. The main industries identified by the UN in the first phase were biomass and food, the manufacturing industry, construction, plastics, and consumer goods. However, the fact that its quality does not decrease when recycled and the fact that it is fully recyclable have made the glass industry a prime example for the circular economy.

Circularity of Glass Industry

Glass, which finds its place in almost every field from agriculture to the health sector, art to renewable energy production, or daily life as packaging, has a wide range of uses due to its functionality, longevity, and no harm to nature and people. With the UN declaring 2022 the year of glass, its global importance was once again emphasized. This importance and wide usage make the circularity of glass mandatory.

One of the main reasons that glass is a prime example in the circular economy is its fully recyclable nature. This feature intensifies the production and use of glass globally. According to the International Commission on Glass, on average, 650 glass container manufacturers produce 95 million tons, 320 flat glass manufacturers produce 106 million tons of flat glass, and 230 manufacturers melt 8 million tons of glass per year. It was assumed that the estimated glass production value is approximately $189 billion and grows by 5.2 % each year (Dyer 2014; International Committee for Museums and Collection of Glass [ICOM] 2021).

The use of refilling and reuse instead of melting, crushing, or remanufacturing in such a large-volume industry would lead to an increase in the profit margins of regional small-scale companies. In addition, raising awareness of consumers making recyclable choices in the purchasing process would have cost-reducing effects (Schandl et al. 2020).

Afterward, it can be reused by melting and shaping, which significantly reduces resource consumption. This is defined in the literature as the completion of circularity in the glass industry. In addition, the fact that its use does not have a negative impact on nature, recycling by melting rather than new production reduces the environmental damage and carbon emissions. Also, recycled glass can be used as an input in different sectors. After being melted and turned into sand, it can be used in road construction as asphalt or can be used as cement (Durán & Parker 2022).

Lin (2018) detailed the benefits of glass recycling as follows:

- 1.2 tons of raw materials are saved because of using 1 ton of recycled glass.
- Recycling 1 ton of glass avoids the production of 175 kilos of waste, thus reducing the cost of landfilling.
- Recycling 1 ton of glass creates 20 % less air pollution.
- Recycling 1 ton of glass creates 50 % less water pollution.

Figure 3.1 represents the levels of collection for recycling rate in percent terms in Europe for the years 2021, 2020, and 2019. Accordingly, collection

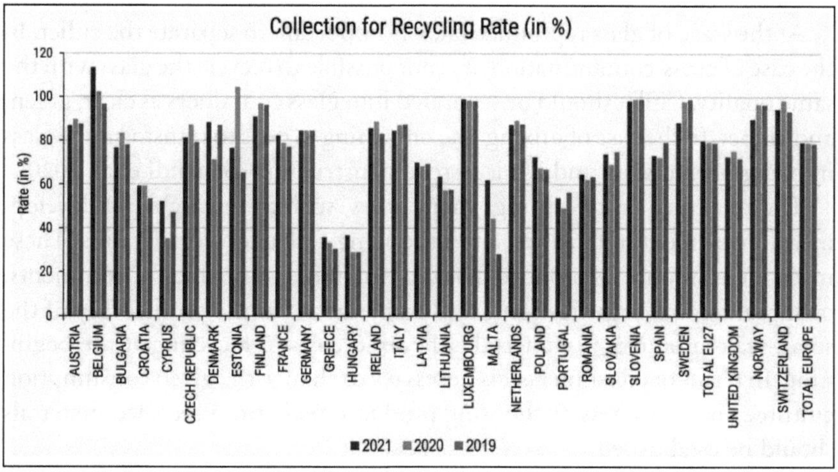

Figure 3.1. Latest available data on the levels of collection for glass recycling.
Source: (Database) www.closetheglassloop.eu

by consumers for recycling has increased over the years. However, this graph, which presents a representative ratio, does not reflect the recycling rates. Although the collection for recycling is 78 % across Europe, only 50 % recovered, and 36 % is used in repackaging. The primary reason for these differences is the ineffectiveness and difficulty of the collection and sorting systems (Schandl et al. 2020).

The existence of a perfectly planned collection system is the first pillar of glass recycling. Properly collected glass is infinitely and completely recyclable without any new raw material usage. This stage of recycling is entirely dependent on consumers and the quality of available collection bins. At this point, the investment of the public–private sectors in recycling becomes important in terms of increasing the sensitivity of consumers through education or incentives and creating quality collection bins.

Sorting is necessary to make the collection more efficient. We need to sort glass successfully. The first condition for successful sorting is that the glass should not be mixed with other raw materials like aluminum during the production process. In addition, thicker glass does not break during the sorting process, and this facilitates recycling so it has a higher chance for the reproduction process.

At the stage of glass reproduction, it is important to separate the cullet. In the case of cross-contamination, it is not possible to recycle the glass with the same quality. Cullet should be separated into glass containers as clear, green, and amber. In the case of mixing, the only thing to do is to transform the glass into engineered sand and use it in road construction (Schandl et al. 2020).

The recycling process brings many costs, such as research and development, investment in facilities, and producing collection-sorting bins. These investments should be supported by multinational companies, governments, or supranational organizations. It is problematic for the profitability of the small-scale producer to undertake the fixed costs of recycling at the beginning. In terms of consumers, it is necessary to change the given consumption culture. The awareness of choosing products made from recycled materials should be established.

Conclusion

Sustainability of the existing resources in the world is endangered due to excessive population growth and the tendency to consume. The traditional economy and the "take-make-dispose" pattern, which costs a lot to the world, are now being replaced by the circular economy, as it could not provide a solution to the problems of the world. The circular economy with 9R strategies (refuse–rethink–reduce–reuse–repair–refurbish–remanufacture–repurpose–recycle–recover) intends to prevent products from becoming pure waste. It aims to reduce the usage of resources, reduce the production costs, and reduce environmental damage by ensuring products are not totally wasted. It reintroduces resources into the economy.

The reason that the glass industry is the most suitable example in this field is that it is fully recyclable, and no waste is produced when recycled. However, as expected, glass recycling is not entirely trouble-free and costless. The primary problem in glass recycling is its collection and sorting. The cooperation of consumers is needed in the collection process of glass. The labeling of glass products at the production stage and the access of individuals to collection bins affect the collection rate. After collecting, the problematic sorting process begins.

To fully recycle without any action to be possible, glass must be unbroken and reusable. If it is damaged, it is necessary to separate the collected glass according to its colors. When this separation is not done properly, the quality of the obtained recycled raw material decreases. In the case of mixing, the only thing to do is to transform the glass into engineered sand and use it in road construction.

In other words, glass never turns into garbage. Even if its quality decreases, it can at least participate in a different production process as raw material (sand).

CHAPTER 4

Direction of Banks in the Digitalizing World

Gökhan Sönmezler

ABSTRACT
This section discusses the effect of the digital transformation accelerated by COVID-19 on banking. The pandemic has accelerated shifts because digital tools are now so vital for maintaining economic activity, and consumers have rapidly flocked to digital banking. The banking sector digitalization has opened up cost-cutting possibilities and, at the same time, threats that raise competition. Technological disruption by FinTech and BigTech companies has out-competed traditional banks with their obsolete technological legacies. Digital opportunities include improved cost efficiency, AI-assisted customized services, and scale. But threats are coming that will reshape the turf: heightened competition, a dilution of brand value, the need to invest in technology, cyberattacks, and the digital divide. The digitalization of business models is altering the nature of banking fundamentally, where future directions in terms of digital competition and countries' technology infrastructures will be closely linked to the fate of this sector.

Keywords: Digitalization, banking sector, FinTech, artificial intelligence, cybersecurity

Jel Codes: G21, O33

Introduction

The COVID-19 pandemic has changed some things in everyone's life. While this change was small in some areas, there were big changes in some areas. The key element in almost all these changes is digital transformation. Today, all electronic devices, such as mobile phones and computers, are digital and use information in digital code. However, the technological infrastructure that played a role in the digital transformation during the pandemic period was developed before the pandemic. In this way, the digitalization of commercial activities and business models, that is, digital transformation, was made possible during the pandemic period (Liu 2021: 6). Thus, thanks to the digital infrastructure created before the pandemic, the transition to digitalization during the pandemic period was also quite fast.

Digital tools have significantly helped in combating diseases and sustaining economic activities during the pandemic. With the spread of the coronavirus, digital transformation has become the main element of continuing economic activities and combating the pandemic. Many economic activities have become digital to comply with social distancing practices. Since the rate of spread of the pandemic is high, consumers have had to move to the digital environment at almost the same speed. In short, COVID has disrupted the old living and working order of society all over the world and created a new process.

The new process that started in the living and working order of society with the pandemic has revealed the need for different organizations for companies and individuals. Because a more customer-oriented structure has emerged in the new process (Sadiku et al. 2022: 233). In this structure, while the role of the young population was more active in the early stages of the pandemic, balancing occurred over time as every segment of the population reached a high level of digital penetration (Hajro et al. 2021: 1). From the perspective of companies, digitalization has accelerated competition by increasing the access of small- and medium-sized companies to the market and increasing the need for operational flexibility of companies. While digitalization has reduced companies' costs on the one hand, it has also brought about the need to use the saved costs in more efficient areas (KPMG 2022: 12). In addition, digital transformation has created a new competitive issue for companies: Digital competition. Because, while the distinction between small and large companies has disappeared for consumers with digital transformation, this development has also reduced brand awareness. In short, this process, which reduces customer loyalty (Abbott 2024: 12), puts companies in an intense competitive environment to increase their awareness in the digital environment.

Digitalization and digital transformation are not actually new issues for companies. Before the pandemic, certain sectors had started to take steps toward digitalization. However, the pandemic process made digitalization necessary for the sustainability of economic activities and accelerated digital transformation. After the pandemic, digital life has become normal in many sectors, and there is no possibility of returning to the pre-pandemic period. At this point, it is now possible for consumers to largely adopt the digital life that has joined their lives during the pandemic and not want to give up this life. However, there are naturally sectoral differences in the adoption of digital services. While this rate is low in some sectors, it may be higher in others. Consumers in the banking sector, which is the subject of our study, adopt online banking services with a high average of 82 % and want to continue using them after the pandemic (Fernandez et al. 2020: 7). Consumer satisfaction obtained from digital banks is higher than that obtained from traditional banks (Alderman & Valenti 2020: 9).

In the banking sector, the rapid and high rate of consumer adoption of online banking applications brings about a rapid change in the sector. Perhaps the developments that will take place in one or a few decades will need to be much faster. This creates significant pressure on the sector. At this point, consumers are much more conscious of digital banking. Consumers who have stepped into digital banking out of necessity during the pandemic period are also increasing their desire for digital banking (Alderman & Valenti 2020: 15).

The Effects of Digitalization on the Financial Sector

The banking sector, which provides financial resources to the real economy, plays a key role in the economic growth of countries. This role is smaller in countries with very strong capital markets, such as the US or the UK, while it is larger in EU countries where capital markets are relatively weak. In countries with strong capital markets, non-financial companies issue debt instruments to access financing, while EU companies rely largely on loans to access financing (Beck et al. 2022: 37). In this respect, developments in the banking sector in the EU are of great importance for the future of countries, as they can affect all other sectors of the countries.

In the financial sector, banks have generally been leaders in adopting many progressive applications, including the implementation of new technologies (Murinde et al. 2022: 2). This is also true for the adoption of digitalization technologies. Digital transformation, which involves the use of digital technologies to transform commercial activities, competencies, and business models, is a much more advanced stage than online banking, which refers to remote access to banks. Digital banking is based on high-level process automation and web-based services and applications to provide banks and their customers with a high level of cost efficiency and flexibility (Malyshev 2023). In this respect, the digital applications that consumers expect from banks have now moved to a much more advanced level than the online banking applications that were sufficient in the early stages of the pandemic. It is possible to see the stages of digitalization in financial processes from Table 4.1. Technological developments supporting innovations in the field of finance have both strengthened and accelerated developments in the financial sector. However, the real big speed explosion occurred in the 2000s with the widespread use of the internet and mobile technologies (Liu 2021: 7–8).

Table 4.1. Two dimensions of financial service digitalization.

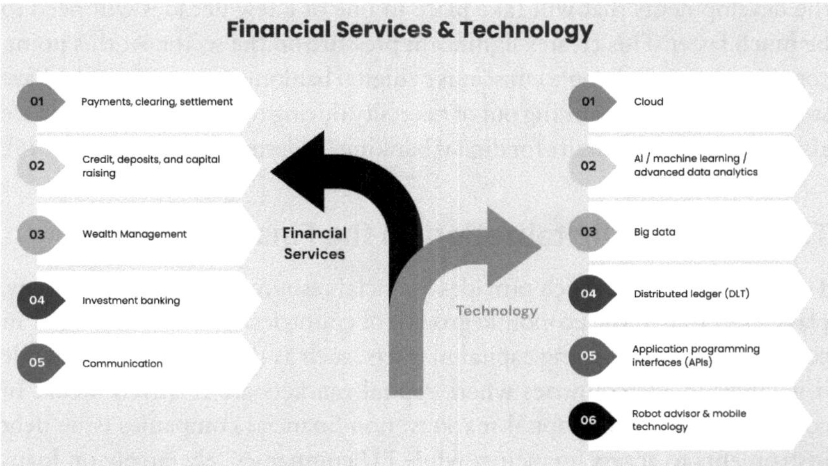

Source: Liu (2021)"Stay Competitive in the Digital Age: The Future of Banks," IMF Working Paper, p. 7.

The leading position of banks in adopting new technologies has eroded somewhat after the global financial crisis. Banks that were damaged by the global financial crisis stayed away from technological investments after the crisis period to repair their balance sheets (Liu 2021: 8). One of the important examples in this regard is the EU banking system. However, the problem of EU banks cannot be explained only by the global financial crisis. The profitability of the EU banking system has been low for the last 40 years. In this system, which also points to other structural problems, EU banks must work with a very old technological infrastructure. Naturally, this situation puts the EU banking system at a disadvantage against potential competitors (Beck et al. 2022: 39). Nevertheless, the existing technological infrastructure has been a lifesaver for the EU banking sector, especially during the pandemic period. Deposits in the EU banking sector continued to increase during the pandemic period, as can be seen from the graph below. In this respect, the EU banking system did not experience significant problems during the pandemic period despite its old technology. However, this does not mean that it will not experience any problems in the future. Technology is a variable that comes before innovative products and distribution channels. Technological developments affect not only products and services but also the production and distribution processes of banking products (Sadiku et al. 2022: 233). In this respect, it is highly probable that banks that lag in technology will also lag in terms of products.

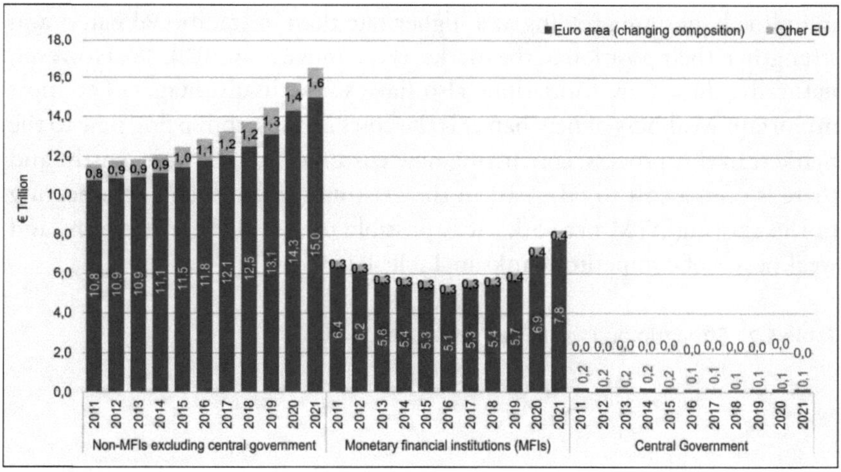

Figure 4.1. Bank deposits in EU.
Source: EBF (2022) Banking in Europe: EBF Facts & Figures 2022, p.12.

The pandemic has been an important test for the financial sector, just like the rest of the world. In this process, where physical interaction was minimized, digitalization was actually a one-way street for the banking sector. However, consumers' adoption of digital banking applications during this period and their desire to use them after the pandemic acted as a catalyst that accelerated the process. However, adapting to digitalization technology was not the only difficulty for banks in the process. The rapidly increasing customer demands and the differentiation between the technological infrastructures of banks and what they could offer caused new competitors such as FinTech and BigTech to enter the sector (Liu 2021: 8). In addition, banks had to compete with these new competitors under very disadvantageous conditions. Because while banks were trying to adapt the old technology applications they used to the new situation with cost-effective operations, their competitors were forming that emerged because of the need for new business models (Murinde et al. 2022: 12).

The strongest aspect of new competitor banks is that consumers are aware of digital transformation and are increasingly demanding in this regard. This creates the opportunity for new formations to quickly acquire customers and grow rapidly by making good use of technological opportunities. Deposits in online banks are growing at a higher rate than in traditional banks and strengthen their position in the market (Fernandez et al. 2020: 28). However, naturally, these new formations also have some disadvantages. The most important weakness of new banks is the costs arising from being new to the market. In this process, convincing new customers can be quite costly, and there is even a cost to take part in the existing system (such as connecting to the existing ATM network). It is possible to see all these strengths and weaknesses of competitor banks in Table 4.2.

Table 4.2. Strengths and weaknesses of challenger banks.

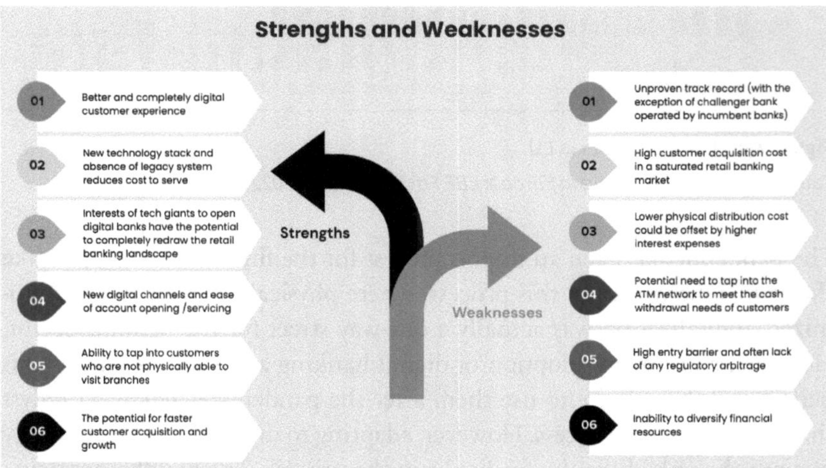

Source: Citi Group (2019) and Murinde et al. (2022).

Rapidly changing customer demands and new competitors entering the market have led traditional banks to differentiate and adapt to the new situation. As can be seen in Figure 4.2, there are differences between the business models of traditional banks and digital banks. The transition from the traditional banking model, which is time-consuming for customers and unattractive for the younger generations and human-intensive, to the more modern and efficient business model of digital banking naturally brings with it opportunities and threats. The opportunities and threats that may arise as a result of banks' digitalization efforts will be discussed in the next section.

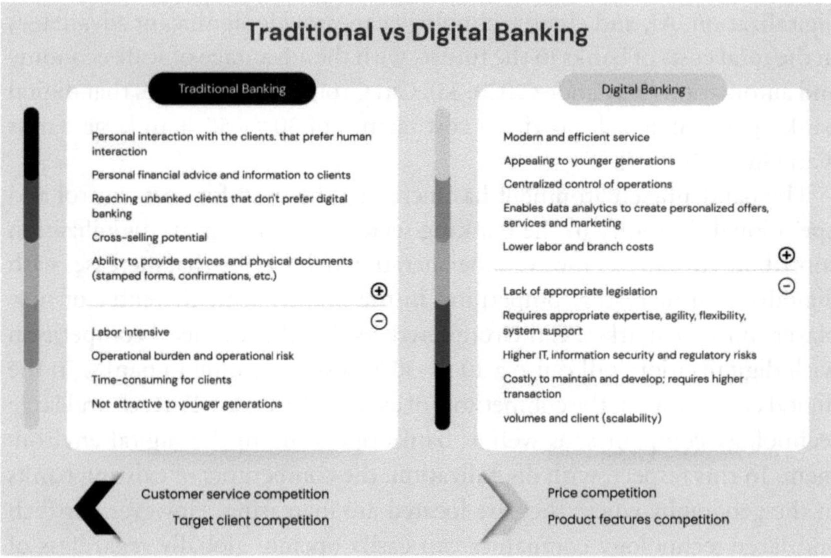

Figure 4.2. Traditional banks versus digital banks.

Digitalization in Banks—Opportunities and Threats

Digitalization is about using technology to increase efficiency and effectiveness in the current environment. In this respect, the first thing that comes to mind in the opportunities that digitalization will create in banks is the decrease in costs. In fact, with COVID, the road to a cashless society has accelerated, and banks have expanded their online services. While consumer transactions can be handled online, internet banks without any physical branches have begun to emerge in the market. These developments have naturally reduced branch operating costs (Sadiku et al. 2022: 234). In addition, the increasing use of artificial intelligence (AI) with digitalization is expected to increase efficiency in the banking sector by 22 %–30 % (Abbott 2024: 5). Digitalization increases efficiency by accelerating front- and back-office transactions and reduces the cost of information processing (Murinde et al. 2022: 4). As a result, technology applications that increase efficiency in banks, technology-supported business models, and thus less labor usage are developments that reduce costs. In addition, the increase in the use of digitalization, AI, and cloud technology can provide significant advantages in the total costs of banks in the future, with the advantage of scale economy and automation (Fernandez 2020: 33). Citi Group also calculates that digital banking activities will provide a cost savings of 30 %–50 % in large banks (Citi Group 2019: 4).

The pandemic environment has increased the need for cost control and operational flexibility in the banking sector. In this respect, digitalization contributes to banks. However, the operational flexibility that increases with digitalization increases competition in the market with the entry of new players into the market. Citi Group predicts that the increased competition with digitalization will cause a 10 %–30 % loss of income in banks. In the digital environment, the competitors of existing banks are FinTech and large technology companies, as well as banks operating in the digital environment. In this respect, with digitalization, the competitors of existing banks in the geography where they are located are increasing. However, FinTech and large technology companies can easily operate globally regardless of the jurisdiction they operate in (Beck et al. 2022: 37). In this respect, since digitalization eliminates physical boundaries, existing banks need to compete with competitors outside their own geography.

The changing business model in the banking sector with digitalization offers opportunities for cost reductions in the future, while it also poses significant threats due to increasing competition conditions. One of the possible threats that digitalization poses to banks in the future is the loss of brand perception, which was also experienced during the pandemic. Transferring business models to the digital environment reduces brand perception by severing the customer–company relationship. The gradual decrease in brand perception with digitalization requires banks to increase their marketing activities to retain their existing customers and acquire new customers.

Marketing activities are an important cost element that can reach up to 25 %–35 % of total operating expenses for a digital bank that has just entered the market. Of course, even if the cost does not reach these points for banks that are already in the market, it can still reach significant figures.

Another factor that increases the costs of banks with digitalization is technology investments. Banks cannot afford to stand still when it comes to technology. Customer demand for the convenience brought by technology will increase (Sadiku et al. 2022: 239). In a way, digital technology is a product that determines the difference between banks and increases competition (Tran et al. 2023: 19). In addition, as digitalization increases in the banking sector, non-bank FinTech or technology companies are also becoming more competitive (Bousrih 2023: 275). In this respect, there is always competition between financial institutions in the field of technology, and today, digitally developed institutions are in a more advantageous position in this competition. Digital banks can respond to customer requests faster by personalizing customer needs (McKinsey 2023: 16). However, while digital transformation in the banking sector improves the performance of banks, a combination of resources and technology is also required to achieve the desired results (Porfírio et al. 2024: 7). At this point, there is a change in human resources along with technology in the banking sector. Change in human resources after the US crisis, the number of full-time employees in the banking sector, which invested in technology for cost optimization, gradually decreased by 7 %–16 %. This change not only remains quantitative but also qualitative. While the number of professional personnel in the sector decreased, the number of technical personnel increased (Citi Group 2019: 25). The new structure also brings about changes in purpose for professional personnel. Because with digitalization, the automation of long-time tasks in the front and back offices will allow existing professional personnel to spend more time on customer interactions (Abbott 2024: 36).

Another factor that may increase costs for banks with digitalization is the source of digital money. Whether digital money is issued by central banks or by private-sector institutions has substantially different implications for the structure of the banking sector. With digital money, it is inevitable for banks to have a more volatile financing base. This structure, which will cause banks to work with shorter-term financing sources, also increases the costs and risks of banks (Beck et al. 2022: 43). A possible threat or source of concern for the banking sector with digitalization is that digital transformation will lead to an unequal distribution of benefits. This concern is valid for countries as well. Digital differences between countries will also affect the growth rates and development levels of countries. Naturally, the difference in development levels also affects banks. However, first, looking at institutions in the same geography will provide a better understanding of the issue.

The banking sector is a sector where concentration is high in terms of structure. In this respect, digitalization has been able to increase concentration in the banking sector due to high initial investment costs (Liu 2021: 10). This situation may lead to some banks reaching higher market power in the domestic banking sector with harmful consequences. In addition, one of the features of digitalization in the banking sector is that it helps overcome physical boundaries. It has become much easier for customers in one country to access financial products suitable for them in a different jurisdiction with the digital transformation. With this development, competition in the domestic sector may increase or, on the contrary, competition may decrease. Large banks in developed countries that quickly realize digital transformation and provide a cost advantage may reduce competition in financial markets in countries that cannot do this (UNCTAD 2022: 41). Comparison between countries shows that digital banking is more widely used in high-income developed countries (Liu 2021: 12). In this case, in the coming years, it may be possible that developed countries, which have implemented digitalization earlier and faster, not only in the banking sector but in all sectors, will rapidly widen the gap between them and developing countries, and that income and social inequality in the world will increase even more. However, while banks lead the advancement of digital finance in high-income countries, the leading role in developing countries is mostly in non-bank structures (Liu 2021: 14). In contrast to the role of large banks in increasing the density in the markets, the role of non-bank structures in increasing competition will determine the future market structure in financial markets. In this respect, the future of the banking sector will differ depending on the market structure in the country in question (OECD 2020: 37). Investments in digital infrastructure to keep the market competitive, a strong business environment with the rule of law, and a healthy competitive environment covering banks and the non-bank FinTech sector will be positive steps for the future (Liu 2021: 26).

With digitalization, the use of AI, which can make a leap in production and customer experiences in the banking sector, has also opened the way. The most important effect of the use of AI in banking is that it is possible to personalize the service provided to customers (McKinsey 2023: 17). Determining products according to people's needs naturally carries the customer's usage experience to a higher profile (KPMG 2022: 6). Although the infrastructure of banks is not currently suitable for full personalization due to the high level of AI use, it is inevitable that customer experience will be better in this regard in the future. Naturally, banks will want to convert the experience they gain through personalization into money. Personalizing products, that is, offering different products to each customer, naturally brings about different prices for these different goods. In this formation, referred to as price differentiation in the literature, the company wants to maximize profits by applying the highest price to customers with different income levels. In this respect, product personalization in the banking sector is an opportunity that can increase market power and therefore profitability.

With the pandemic, the transition to digitalization in the banking sector has accelerated, as we have previously stated. In this respect, the pandemic has brought many consumers to an environment that is not very hospitable and has many question marks about security (UNCTAD 2022: 41). Digitalization has increased non-financial risks under the umbrella of operational risks in the banking system. Cyberattacks and governance problems can cause data breaches, the jeopardization of the private data of millions of customers, and high fraud costs (Fernandez et al. 2020: 33). Bank customers are already aware of this risk, and participants in the Deloitte study state that they will use digital products more if data security is increased (Alderman & Valenti 2020: 9). Banks are caught between the increasing demands of customers in this direction with digitalization and the increasing data security risks in the digitalized world. At this point, banks will face an important test for a successful digitalization strategy. Banks will need to create their own digital DNA for a cost-effective, fast, personal, and risk-free structure.

Conclusion

Digitalization in the banking sector has occurred very quickly and somewhat unscheduled. This situation, which stems from the pandemic environment, brings both some opportunities and some risks to the sector. The most important advantage of increasing digitalization for banks seems to be the decrease in costs and the positive impact it will have on future profitability. However, this is not an easy process. Because digitalization increases market competition by influencing new competitors to enter the market, while on the other hand, the rapid growth environment realized with digitalization increases the market power of some banks. From this perspective, the banking market seems to be shaped between these two developments in the coming periods. The future of the sector will be determined by the structure in which the market will evolve because of these two developments.

CHAPTER 5

An Introduction to Distributed Ledger Technology (DLT)

Semih Köksal & İsmail Orçun Gündüz

ABSTRACT

In this paper, we review the basic principles of DLT, which originates from the data architecture of the internet, to study its working and application in financial markets. The historical development of information storage and transfer instruments is clarified, leading to the identification of DLT as a novel data structure. Comparison of these structures with the secure DLT facilitation characteristics is prepared through considering torrent-like decentralized data distribution models aimed at facilitating secure transactions devoid of intermediaries, block transactions, and wallet addresses. The implications of allowing for the fractionalized ownership that the digital minting of tokens and non-fungible tokens (NFTs) would have on the financial markets is analyzed. The capabilities of smart contracts to cut operational costs by automating the traditional front-office (FO), middle-office (MO), and back-office (BO) processes are assessed as well as the cost-cutting and liquidity-enhancing properties that were brought by the tokenization of securities—with a special focus on bond markets—finally, ... the literature was reviewed in relation to the latter subject. Results show that DLT could establish a new financial platform for public and private, simultaneously contributing to enhanced financial transactions transparency, traceability, and cost reduction. But it is emphasized that there are technicalities, such as a lack of interoperability across platforms, and risks with the smart contract have to be sorted out.

Keywords: Distributed ledger technology (DLT), tokenization and NFTs, smart contracts, peer-to-peer (P2P) transactions, security tokenization

Jel Codes: G32, O33

Introduction

The power of knowledge and know-how has determined the welfare of societies in every stage of history, while also determining their fate in future generations. As a concept, knowledge, in its broadest definition, is an inference obtained through intellectual activity on experience or fact. The system formed by adding these inferences to each other constitutes know-how. With this system, individuals and societies redesign, organize, and develop their production (Fazey et al. 2020).

Writing, which is our first information recording and transfer system born from the human ability to speak and think, began, as far as is known, with the drawing of simple pictures and geometric shapes on small stones in the Paleolithic age. Subsequently, cuneiform, which was written on clay tablets by the Sumerians in Mesopotamia around 4000 BC to record economic relations, emerged. With the invention of paper in China and its subsequent spread in the European continent, the storage and transfer of information became easier, and in the twentieth century, transistors, which developed with the discovery of electricity, opened the doors to the ability to store and transfer information as well as to perform calculations outside the human mind. Computers, consisting of millions of transistors, have become the new and indispensable information storage tool of modern society due to their ability to store and process huge amounts of information relative to their size. Subsequently, by connecting computers in different parts of the world to each other with the help of cables, the most widespread and up-to-date internet emerged (Goda & Kitsuregawa 2020).

In each advancing era, societies that developed the means of storing and transferring information also sought ways to process this mass of data more effectively, along with the increasing mass of information. The information storage tools used (paper, computers, etc.) have also produced their own data storage–processing structure, depending on the material properties and current technological advances. For example, pages emerged by writing information on paper, books emerged by bringing the information on pages together in a certain order and relationship, and libraries emerged as a total structure classified by clustering books according to a certain relevance. When we go to the library, the totality of the categories and numbering we use to reach the information we are looking for essentially indicates a data structure. Although a library where books are stored randomly and in a complex manner and a library divided into sections and shelves are the same in terms of information capacity, a random and complex library has almost no usefulness. The difference here arises from whether the same information (i.e., data) is organized with a structure. If we call this organization a data structure, developing technological opportunities offers us not only better storage tools but also more effective data structures. In other words, because of this historical development from small stones to computers, the need for the capacity to organize and process data more effectively has increased.

The need to record and transfer information in world history has developed under the influence of the sustainability of economic and financial activities, as well as in different areas. Recording and monitoring economic and financial activities in a region or society in a specific data structure and processing them has become a necessity for the continuation of activities. In particular, the currencies and commodities/assets that are the subject of the modern financial sector are recorded and maintained in accordance with different standards determined by the authorities. Money, which is the subject of financial and economic activities, has become a tool that is used less and less physically and in cash today and is mostly used in a registered form. This situation changes the perspective on money in terms of data structure. The fact that money and assets are basically processed and monitored as numbers in accounting books indicates that the financial system is built on a global data structure. In other words, the entirety of the activities carried out by banks and financial institutions consists of systematically recording the transfer of ownership between individuals and institutions in terms of data. Almost all transactions, such as money transfers from one account to another, buy–sell transactions in domestic and international markets, and customer deposits, are data transactions that are mostly accounted for in a digital environment. For this reason, the development of financial activities and their becoming more sustainable are directly related to the data structure used.

At this point, the question of how the internet, which refers to computers sharing and processing information with each other, will be organized with a data structure has become an important milestone in terms of both sustainability and efficiency. As mentioned in the previous example, how a data stack is organized is a fundamental factor that determines the usefulness of that data stack, and this pushes the internet protocol (IP) to be rebuilt more efficiently. Ultimately, understanding that the internet is also a data structure is the first step in developing its use in sectors such as finance, banking, and the production chain. Although there have been studies on new data structures in the fields of computer science and mathematics since the 1960s, the most global development on this subject was Bitcoin, published and developed in 2009 by a person/group with the pseudonym Satoshi Nakamoto (2008) with the article "Bitcoin: A Peer-to-Peer Electronic Cash System." Contrary to the widespread opinion, blockchain technologies such as Bitcoin are not simple digital money, but a new internet data structure model that can store value. The main purpose of this new data structure model is to minimize the risks and the complexity arising from the centralized data structure of the current internet/local network. In addition, with DLT, the need for intermediary institutions and processes in many sectors can be eliminated and become more transparent, sustainable, and secure. Recording, processing, and reporting of processes in many areas, from the financial sector to industrial production, can be transferred to a "self-monitoring" structure with DLT.

This article examines the basic principles and application areas of DLT technology. Based on basic information about the operation and architecture of the internet, the working principles of DLT and blockchain technologies based on peer-to-peer (P2P) transaction logic are discussed. The role of DLT, which is exemplified especially through distributed data distribution architectures such as Torrent, in tokenization and security tokenization processes is discussed.

First Step: Understanding the Internet

To understand concepts such as blockchain technology and security tokenization, it is necessary to first understand the internet. As mentioned before, DLT or internet technology is a data structure that ultimately determines how existing data will be organized, processed, and stored. Tokenization of securities naturally requires a network on which financial data can be transferred, stored, and organized, and a data structure of this network (network protocol). For this reason, the network needed for the process of tokenizing securities is planned to be established on the existing internet infrastructure in hardware. In other words, since technologies such as DLT that allow tokenization of securities are data structure technologies, they require a network on which the structure will be constructed, and this network, in its broadest form, is the internet.

As its name suggests, the internet refers to the common connection created by connections between networks on a global scale. What is meant by connection here is, in the simplest terms, the ability to share data between two machines. These machines are physically connected to each other. Today, over 98 % of the internet is provided via thousands of kilometers of cables buried under the sea and the ground. In her book Undersea Network, where New York University Dr. Nicole Starosielski discusses these cables, the technology behind them, and their economic and strategic importance, she states that 99 % of all intercontinental internet data flow in the world is provided via these cables, not satellites (Figure 5.1) (Bakırcı 2015).

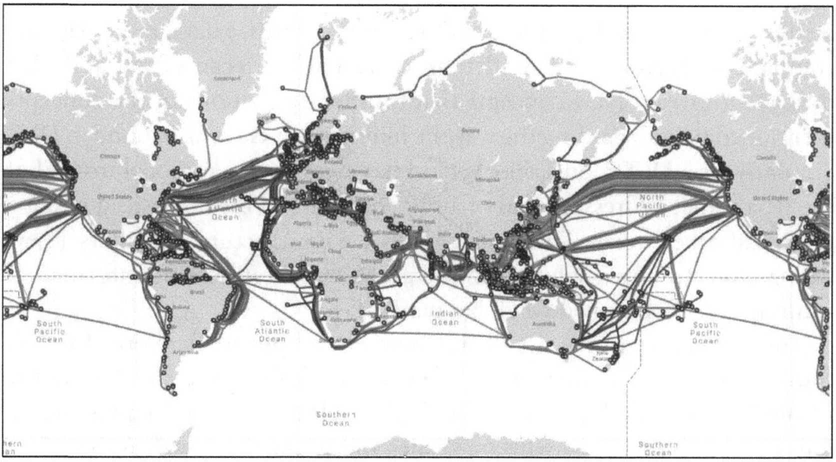

Figure 5.1. Map of oceanic internet cables.
Source: Bakırcı (2015: Nisan 13). Evrim Ağacı. https://evrimagaci.org/okyanus-alti-internet-kablolari-haritasi-3519

In other words, the internet connection that comes to our home or office is made possible by the cables that are pulled up to the floor of the building we are in. Although wireless data sharing technologies are very advanced, we still need physical cable connections to properly operate a structure with huge transaction per second (tps) rates like the internet.

Although the hardware infrastructure of the internet allows computers to share data with each other, as mentioned before, it is not sufficient for a secure infrastructure. A common agreement (protocol) is needed for anonymous parties to be able to interact with each other securely and effectively on a global scale. The protocol in question provides common instructions for computers connected to each other via wires and wirelessly to communicate securely and effectively. In addition, thanks to these instructions, computers that use different languages use a common language. The totality of these instructions is called IP. According to IP instructions, each device connected to the internet has an IP address, and thanks to this address, the address coordinates of the sought information or target interaction are determined without confusion. Moreover, according to the IP, data are transferred via data packets called datagrams. The header of each datagram contains the destination and source addresses, and the payload contains the message to be transmitted. Thanks to these and similar standards, a datagram-receiving computer analyses whether the data are correct, where it came from, and what message it carries. New concepts that fulfill the functions of the concepts mentioned so far regarding the way the internet works are also found in DLT. Similarly, as a DLT model, blockchain has a consensus protocol instead of the IP, a wallet address instead of an IP address, and blocks instead of datagrams. In other words, DLT is essentially a data structure and offers a new data architecture as a solution to the problem of transferring information securely and effectively on a global network.

The acceptance of the use of the internet and private networks for data transfer in traditional financial markets theoretically opens the door to the possibility of using DLT-like technologies. Ultimately, DLT represents an internet that is regulated with new rules and thus gains new features.

One of the basic principles in DLT is to provide secure information transfer between parties within the data structure without the need for a third party. What is meant by security here is the accuracy, confidentiality, and denial of malicious intervention against third parties. The basic logic here is very simple: Records of a system are distributed to the members of the system as identical copies. These copies can be called ledgers. Then, let's say that all transactions within the system are recorded simultaneously in the ledgers held by all members. At this point, even if a malicious member makes a change in his own ledger, that information is not valid since that change is not recorded in the ledgers of the remaining members. The accuracy and validity of the transactions made are ensured if they are recorded by the other members of the system. Under these conditions, the only requirement to perform a malicious transaction is to obtain the majority of the members' ledgers, which is almost impossible. At this point, it should not be forgotten that DLT is formed by the combination of different algorithms in a way that complies with issues such as information privacy, anonymity between parties, and internal information privacy.

An Example Data Distribution Architecture: Torrent

The internet we use in daily life is asymmetrical in terms of its structure. The information on the websites, blogs, or pages we access via the internet is stored on central servers. When we enter a website, we essentially download the information we want to see to our own computer. The fact that more than one person wants to access a website stored on a server at the same time forms the basis of this asymmetry. For this reason, while traditional internet infrastructure often limits download capacity, it provides a wider bandwidth on the upload side. This situation creates inefficiency because multiple users who want to access the same data try to download data from the same server. In addition, in such a system, the source server must be constantly active and have a large output bandwidth. Likewise, if the server where the information is stored and made available for access is not active, people cannot connect to this server, and since this information is not stored on an alternative server other than the relevant server, users cannot access the information. A wide bandwidth is very important for the server to provide a regular and sustainable access service. In a situation where multiple people are trying to download data from a single server at the same time, the server does not have a wide output band means that the server cannot meet the data download demand. In this respect, the Torrent IP is the redesign of the mentioned inefficiency problems by addressing them in terms of data architecture. Basically, the parties share data among themselves with a certain protocol without the need for central servers, thus minimizing the inefficiencies in accessing data.

The origin of the torrent system dates to its development by Bram Cohen in 2001. Cohen aimed to overcome the limitations of existing P2P networks to increase efficiency in file sharing. The torrent system allows a file to be divided into small pieces and distributed among various users, and then, these pieces are reassembled to create the original file (Yang et al. 2008). In other words, the torrent system was created to relieve the load on central servers. Instead of individual clients (computers) downloading files from the server, torrent reduces the time required to download large files by providing the necessary bandwidth through crowdsourcing. It does this by dividing the files into small pieces and distributing them among various users, and then, these pieces are reassembled to create the original file (Yang et al.,2008).

As an important example of the capacity increases produced by the decentralization of data storage–processing–sharing capabilities, the torrent system is similar in principle to DLT. Even for more sensitive data and data that requires access restrictions, it is possible to redesign decentralized systems to benefit from this efficiency increase. In fact, at this point, an important difference for us between torrent systems and DLT systems is data privacy and sensitivity. While torrent systems aim to share public data more efficiently, certain DLT systems aim to establish a decentralized system with the same efficiency for sensitive and confidential data.

DLT and Blockchain: P2P Transaction

Humanity's struggle with nature is a concept integrated with its own existence. Since the early stages of history, humankind, which has spent time and energy to process natural resources and increase its own welfare to survive in nature, has had to exchange the goods and services it has in excess with other goods and services. This "transaction" in which it exchanges the goods and services it has in excess with the goods and services it needs is called barter trade. The oldest known barter trade dates back to 6000 BC. Barter, adopted by Mesopotamian societies, was eventually used by the Phoenicians and Babylonians. During this period, communes increased their welfare by exchanging the products they needed, such as tea, leather, and weapons, among themselves (Nar 2019). Although the economic structure that developed over time established more organized and centralized trade centers and almost eliminated the relatively inefficient barter method, it still constitutes the basic idea of trade. On the other hand, the concept of a "peer-to-peer" (P2P) transaction can be considered almost the same as a barter or exchange transaction. Just like in a barter or exchange, in a P2P transaction, two parties exchange the "things" each other needs by agreeing on a certain rate. These transactions can include various transactions, such as a title deed sale or the exchange of two currencies. The important point is that the transactions can take place between two parties without the need for a third party.

The most basic principle of a barter or exchange transaction is that both parties to the exchange must have the products each other needs. Otherwise, exchange cannot take place. Economists call this condition necessary for exchange to take place "double coincidence of wants." This term was first used in the nineteenth century by British economist William Stanley Jevons (1875) in his book Money and the Mechanism of Exchange. He described this term as the first and most important difficulty of the barter economy. According to Jevons, "The first difficulty in barter is to find two people whose disposable assets mutually fit each other's needs. There may be many people who want and have what is wanted; but there must be mutual coincidence, which is rare, to allow barter." In other words, in any market, the buyer and seller must agree for any given transaction (Hasan 2021). With a very simple mathematical approach, the possibility of "mutual coincidence" required by barter trade can be expanded with a crowded and more accessible context. Our existing technological infrastructure is essentially equipped to enable different buyers and sellers from all over the world to come to terms with each other and be informed of their demands, via the internet. The fundamental problem here is how to ensure trust between the parties in any P2P transaction.

P2P transactions are different from over-the-counter transactions. While there is an intermediary (broker) to reach an agreement between the buyer and seller in over-the-counter transactions, P2P transactions occur directly between the buyer and seller. Although it would be ideal for assets to be transferred directly between individuals, technological and organizational deficiencies to date have forced financial transactions to be conducted by intermediary institutions. Buyers and sellers with different legal scopes, mistrust between the parties, market risk, and credit risk are some of the main reasons for this necessity. At this point, a P2P transaction performed over DLT systems is almost free of these disadvantages. The parties publish the transactions they will perform as a common "smart contract," and the contract enters into force at the point where both parties approve (sign). Moreover, the contract already has the capacity to execute the terms of the contract without allowing any third-party intervention, depending on its design. In other words, when the parties agree on the terms and sign the contract, the fulfillment of the contract terms is guaranteed not by the parties but by the DLT system. Trust between the parties is established through the laws of mathematics and physics.

Token and NFT: Ability to Fractionalize

A very interesting historical event is narrated in the article "The Island of Stone Money" written by F. Milton in 1991. American anthropologist William Henry Furness (1910) III, who spent a few months with the local people on the island of Yap, one of the Caroline Islands off the Pacific Ocean north of New Guinea in 1903, tells the following story about the island economy in his book of the same name: On the island, which had no metal mines in its natural resources, the islanders used an interesting method to conduct trade and daily economic activities among themselves; "fei stones." A type of limestone, which was not one of the natural resources of the Caroline Islands, was processed on another island 400 km away, turned into disks with holes in the middle, and brought to the island with the help of small boats and canoes. These stones, whose sizes ranged from 5–10 cm to 3.5 m, formed the basis of trade in the island economy. Since the large stones were too heavy to be traded, ownership information was changed instead of the physical location of the stones for trade. On this island, where larger stones were more valuable, since everyone knew who owned the large stones and they could not be moved, they served as a "medium of exchange" without the need for storage. The assurance of the ownership of large stones was provided by the fact that all the islanders knew who owned the stone. In fact, this trust mechanism had advanced so much that once a very large and high-quality stone was brought to the island from another island and was buried under the seabed due to a severe storm. However, when they returned to the island, it was confirmed by different witnesses how large and high-quality the stone was, and that the owner of the stone was not at fault, and the owner of the stone and his family became one of the richest families on the island. Moreover, the ownership of this stone under the sea continued to be transferred to his heirs for three generations (Friedman 1991; Türkiye Blockchain Platform 2024).

The trust mechanism mentioned in this historical story constitutes the basic idea of the trust mechanism of DLT and blockchain technologies. The accuracy and security of the transaction between two computers—two clients—is ensured by the "witnessing" of the transaction by other computers. In addition, the "Fei stones" mentioned are conceptually equivalent to the tokens we mentioned in DLT systems. However, as mentioned in the "Torrent network" example, it is still possible to maintain a data-transaction sharing network without an incentive mechanism. However, the development and self-creation of this network is based on volunteering since there is no incentive. Such networks can be called "rewardless networks." On the other hand, an incentive mechanism is added to the DLT network for the development and expansion of the DLT network. Such networks can be called "rewarded networks." The situation of a rewarded–rewardless network is entirely a preference situation regarding the purpose of use of the DLT network to be used. At this point, there are no digital assets such as "coins" and "tokens" in non-rewarded networks, and the main purpose is to create a decentralized information sharing/processing system without trust (see torrent). In rewarded networks, there are two types of digital assets called "coins" and "tokens." By technical definition, "coins" and "tokens" represent similar but different concepts. In a DLT or blockchain system, the digital value produced as an incentive mechanism established for the maintenance of the system is called a coin, while in an existing DLT network, the digital values produced to represent a separate ownership/partnership in a service or project are called "tokens." The distinction here is like the relationship between money and stocks/titles in our traditional economic system. While coins fulfill the basic "medium of exchange" function of the DLT network, tokens are digital assets that represent the ownership/partnership of assets such as stocks or title deeds. For this reason, while there is a limited number of coin types (usually one) in a network, there can theoretically be an infinite number of token types. For a more understandable classification, Figure 5.2 can be examined.

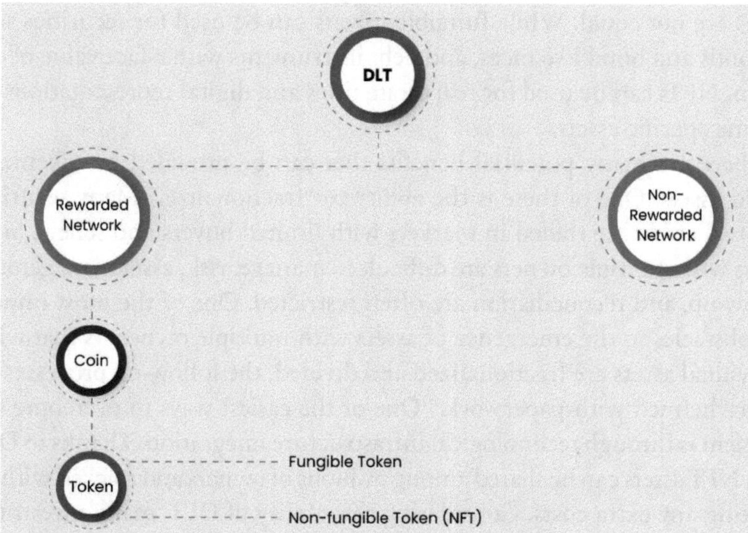

Figure 5.2. DLT diagram.
Source: Hashimy and Sandner (2020)

As shown in Figure 5.2, tokens are examined in two different categories according to their features: Fungible tokens and NFTs. In daily life, while some assets are traded in the markets as identical to each other, some assets are traded specifically as unique assets. For example, for the same type of metal or paper money, each unit is equal and equivalent to another unit, and rather than representing a single asset in a certain coordinate, they represent all values in the same type and unit. On the other hand, a plot of land or real estate is not identical to or equivalent to another real estate. For example, real estates may have different values depending on their different features, such as location and frontage size, and each real estate carries a separate asset representation document (title) unique to itself. At this point, since "fungible" tokens are equal and equivalent to each other, they are like money or lots of stocks of the same company. Just as one lot of X shares of any X company is equal and equivalent to another lot of X shares, the same type of Y token is equal and equivalent to another Y token. NFTs, on the other hand, are similar in design to real estate titles or artworks, as they represent a specific asset at a specific coordinate. In other words, just as two separate real estate titles have different values, or two different paintings are not equivalent, two different NFTs are not equal. While fungible tokens can be used for securities such as bonds and bond issuances, and debt instruments with a face value of one token, NFTs can be used for real estate titles and digital representations for trading specific assets.

There are many potential benefits that can be provided by tokenizing world assets. One of these is the ability to "fractionalize." Many securities and real estate are traded in markets with limited buyers and sellers. Since assets with multiple owners are difficult to manage, risk, asset management, follow-up, and reconciliation are often restricted. One of the most important obstacles to the emergence of assets with multiple owners is that when individual assets are fractionalized and divided, the follow-up processes are "overwhelmed with paperwork." One of the easiest ways to overcome this problem is through technological infrastructure integration. Thanks to DLT, even NFT assets can be shared among millions of owners and tracked without creating any extra costs. Considering this ability of DLT, many investment vehicles from the public sector to private sector assets can be offered to the public without creating extra costs. In other words, it can provide individuals with the ability to fund large infrastructure investments such as hospitals, schools, and bridges in their own city cheaply and quickly, while it can also open the opportunity to invest in public or private debt instruments in another country within seconds at relatively low costs.

Smart Money and Smart Contract: Self-Monitoring System

Despite the advancement of computer technologies to date, when it comes to financial systems, the integration of computers into financial systems is progressing very slowly. The integration of current computer systems into financial systems is progressing slowly due to certain concerns and risks. These concerns and risks may arise from operational risks, reconciliation difficulties, and legal regulations. At this point, although financial operations are carried out through computers, they are still carried out based on human power. On the other hand, computer systems operate according to the laws of physics and mathematics. Through the DLT network, the digital representation of financial assets and values at one point transforms commodities—money—into a programmable entity as an element of the information system cluster. For this reason, money that gains digital representation is conceptually called "smart money." Thanks to smart money, almost all financial transactions that exist can theoretically be subject to digital contracts and programming. These digital contracts are "smart contracts" by definition. The biggest advantage of smart contracts is that they can be executed without the need for trust between the parties. Ultimately, since the goods/currencies that are the subject of the contract are tokenized and transferred to a digital context, the smart contract itself can execute these goods impartially by making them part of its own algorithm. In other words, it consists of code pieces that are written jointly and come into force only when all parties sign them, cannot be silenced except by agreement of the parties after entering into force, and automatically provide the contract terms.

To evaluate the potential advantages of smart contracts more concretely, a classic trade process can be examined. There are three types of offices in conventional treasury transactions: FO, MO, and BO. The FO is the part where traders are located, and the "trade execution"–"trade capture" stages are carried out. The MO is responsible for the reconciliation of the transactions carried out by traders with their counterparty. At this point, the MOs of the two parties meet with each other and provide reconciliation on the details of the transaction. The BO is responsible for the follow-up of the contracts after the transaction, transfer, and payment transactions. Since there is no common structure in this conventional system, each trader has their own MO and BO, and the transaction confirmation is repeated multiple times, increasing the time and manpower cost. Moreover, as a natural result of the lack of a common structure, traders need brokers to share and store information. At this point, the cost points as a whole system increase. On the other hand, separate BO and MO are not needed in the trade cycle carried out with smart contracts. After the trade capture and trade execution stages are performed by the traders, the remaining eight stages are performed automatically by the smart contract with a much lower margin of error. Since the smart contract (unsigned) will not work due to its structure, the agreement is automatically performed between the traders. This situation is a kind of system where the treasuries involved use a single common but granular MO and BO. BO is integrated with FO transactions by automation, and human error is minimized. On the other hand, the number of unnecessary repeated transactions in the entire system is reduced by the partnership. Moreover, since the DLT network is a dynamic structure, it facilitates risk management and reporting processes by allowing dynamic reporting instead of static reporting. The organizational difference between the conventional trade cycle and the DLT trade cycle can be examined in Figure 5.3.

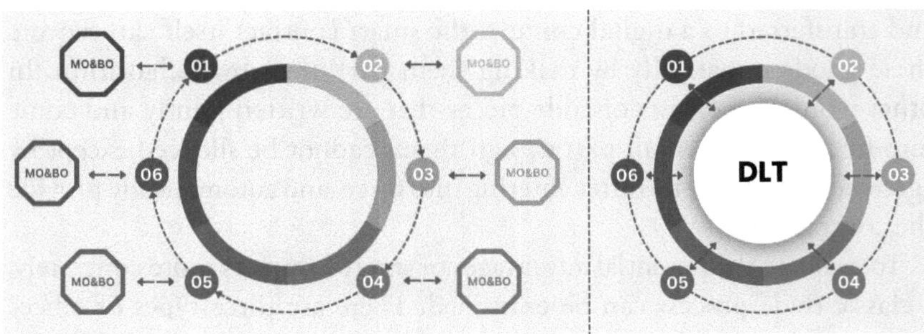

Figure 5.3. Conventional trade cycle (left) and DLT trade cycle (right).
Source: Köksal 2023

Smart contracts still carry technical risks at a technological level. These smart contracts are created on DLT from pre-prepared function and code directories. Tokenized assets on the DLT network operate through these smart contracts. The potential openness and errors that code may contain may lead to problems that are difficult to fix if they are not tested at a sufficient level. At this point, empirical studies are needed to ensure that DLT networks and smart contracts that can be used at the financial institution level can provide lower operational risk claims.

The representation of assets is not only physical, but can be made more reliable, faster, and adaptable with the help of technological infrastructures. Although the "Fei stones mechanism" on the island of Yap sounds dysfunctional and cumbersome, a digitalized version of the same mechanism has the potential to open the way for new opportunities and capabilities in the world of financial capital. With the digital representation of assets and smart contracts, the reconciliation time and costs required by trust will gradually decrease.

Security Tokenization

Tokenization offers an innovative approach that enables secure, P2P transactions in bond markets, powered by DLT. The decentralized structure of DLT establishes trust between parties while minimizing the need for intermediary institutions in bond issuance and management processes. Lowering the barrier to entry in bond issuance processes can play an important role in decentralizing capital. According to Wright (2020), the minimum denomination is reduced from $5,000 to $5 to $10, while the cost per transaction is 0.00035 %, which is an acceptable cost point. The reduced denomination will increase market access and liquidity by increasing the ease of access to the market (Wright 2020). Malamas et al. (2020) emphasized that blockchain technology can provide traceability, security, and cost-effectiveness in green bond issuance. The study proposes a system using smart contracts based on the ERC-20 token standard for tracking investments in green projects. There are four different roles in the five-step DLT-based bond issuance model presented in the study: Issuer, Validator, Regulator, and Investor. The Issuer is responsible for the creation and management of digital bonds, transparent submission of impact reports, and the realization of coupon payments at specified intervals. In addition, reliability can be increased by integrating external audits. While the Validator verifies the issuer's impact reports on the project, compliance with the framework, and fulfillment of commitments, the Regulator has the authority to intervene if any irregularities are detected in the block formation by monitoring the consensus between the parties. Investors can create and manage their portfolios and monitor the performance of their assets by discovering new investment opportunities within this ecosystem.

Another important study on security tokenization is the report conducted by the Hong Kong Institute for Monetary and Financial Research (2023). The report analyses the potential benefits of bond tokenization and examines significant reductions in transaction costs due to the transfer and automation of bond issuance to digital platforms. In addition, the study reveals that liquidity can be increased and the need for intermediary institutions can be reduced. It was found that tokenized bonds have an average of 0.22 % lower underwriting cost and 0.78 % lower borrowing cost. Moreover, it was stated that tokenized bonds have a lower bid-ask spread (5.3 %), and this spread increases to 10.8 % when opened to retail investors (Hong Kong Institute for Monetary and Financial Research 2023). The study suggests that tokenized bonds are more advantageous than traditional bonds in terms of both cost efficiency and market liquidity (Efdata.org).

Barnes (2020) examines existing architectures and smart contract languages on the portability of tokenized assets. The study addresses the factors affecting the portability of tokens between different distributed ledgers and evaluates how adequate the existing technological infrastructures are in this regard. As a result of this review, it reveals that different DLT platforms are not compatible with each other, and this incompatibility limits the portability of tokenized assets. The study also proposes a portability maturity model as a method of assessing portability. This model provides a usable metric for assessing the current state of the technology and market infrastructure. The portability of tokenized assets is a critical factor for the wider adoption of distributed ledger technologies in the financial services sector. Barnes (2020) suggests that existing architectures and technologies are limited in terms of portability, but that future developments in this area can make significant contributions to the widespread use of tokenization.

Conclusion

DLT, one of the most recent products of advanced information technologies, can be considered as a technology that has the potential to re-establish many forms of organization, from social organizations to financial markets. The use of this technology as a public and private sector financing tool can improve direct investment mechanisms. For example, while local governments provide direct public expenditures through municipal bonds, the use of tokenized bonds can increase investment in traceable local assets and improve transparency in public expenditures (Wright 2020). Considering this current information, DLT has great potential as a financing tool. It is obvious that more empirical data are needed for the usability of this technology in sensitive information areas such as finance. With increasing empirical data and enterprise experiences globally, DLT sheds light on the way to create market mechanisms that are more transparent and converge to fully competitive market conditions.

Bibliography

Abbas, S., and Halog, A. (2021). 'Analysis of Pakistani Textile Industry: Recommendations Towards Circular and Sustainable Production'. In *Circular Economy: Assessment and Case Studies*, pp. 77–111. Singapore: Springer Singapore.

Abbott, M. (2024). 'Banking of AI', Accenture, pp. 1–46, https://www.accenture.com/content/dam/accenture /final/industry/banking/document/Accenture-Banking-Top-10-Trends-2024.pdf.

Alderman, R., and Valenti, J. (2020) 'Building on the Digital Banking Momentum', Deloitte, pp. 1–18, https://www2.deloitte.com/content/dam/insights/articles/us134194_cfs-digital-banking-stick/DI_CFS-digital-banking.pdf.

Arner, D. W., Barberis, J., and Buckley, R. P. (2015). *The Evolution of FinTech: A New Post-Crisis Paradigm? University of New South Wales Law Research Series*, https://doi.org/10.2139/ssrn.2676553.

Asante, R., Daniel, F., Martin, A., and Sharfuddin, A. K. (2022). 'Life Cycle Stage Practices and Strategies for Circular Economy: Assessment in Construction and Demolition Industry of an Emerging Economy', *Environmental Science and Pollution Research*, 29 (54), 82110–82121.

Assembly General. (2025). 'Resolution Adopted by the General Assembly on 25 September 2015', United Nations.

Bakırcı, Ç. M. (2015). 'Okyanus altı internet kabloları haritası. Evrim Ağacı', https://evrimagaci.org/okyanus-alti-internet-kablolari-haritasi-3519.

Barnes, R. (2020). 'Factors in the Portability of Tokenized Assets on Distributed Ledgers', *ArXiv*, https://doi.org/10.12345/arxiv.abcdef.

Beck, T., Cecchetti, S., Grothe, M., Kemp, M., Pelizzon, L., and Sánchez Serrano, A. (2022). *Will Video Kill the Radio Star? Digitalisation and the*

Future of Banking (Reports of the Advisory Scientific Committee No. 12). European Systemic Risk Board, https://www.esrb.europa.eu/pub/asc/reports/html/index.en.html.

Bousrih, J. (2023). 'The Impact of Digitalization on the Banking Sector: Evidence from Fintech Countries', *Asian Economic and Financial Review*, 13 (4), 269–278.

Blok, V. (2023). 'The Ontology of Technology Beyond Anthropocentrism and Determinism: The Role of Technologies in the Constitution of the (post)Anthropocene World', *Found Science* 28, 987–1005, https://doi.org/10.1007/s10699-022-09829-1.

Canikli, S. (2022). 'Sustainable Finance Mechanisms and Sustainable Development Relationship', *Akdeniz İİBF Journal*, 22 (1), 26–39, https://doi.org/10.25294/auiibfd.903364.

Chen, J., and Zhang, L. (2020). 'Blockchain in the Finance Industry: Innovations and Challenges', *Journal of Financial Innovation*, 5 (2), 23–45.

Chobanova, R. (2020). 'Circular Economy as a New Stage of Economic Development'. In *Circular Economy – Recent Advances, New Perspectives and Applications*. IntechOpen.

Citi Group. (2019). '"Bank X: The New New Banks." Citi GPS: Global Perspectives and Solutions"', https://www.citigroup.com/global/insights/citigps/bank-x-new-new-banks.

Cunha, F. A. F. S., Meira, E., and Orsato, R. J. (2021). 'Sustainable Finance and Investment: Review and Research Agenda', *Business Strategy and the Environment*, 30 (8), 3821–3838, https://doi.org/10.1002/bse.2842.

Demirgüç-Kunt, A., Klapper, L., Singer, D., Ansar, S., and Hess, J. (2018). *The Global Findex Database 2017: Measuring Financial Inclusion and the FinTech Revolution.* Washington, DC: World Bank Publications.

Durán, A., and Parker, J. M. (2022). *Welcome to the Glass Age: Celebrating the United Nations International Year of Glass.* Madrid: CSIC.

Dünya. (2024). 'Tokenizasyon ve DeFi: Geleneksel Finansın Yeniden Tanımlanması', https://www.dunya.com/kose-yazisi/tokenizasyon-ve-defi-geleneksel-finansin-yeniden-tanimlanmasi/.

Dyer, M., Wu, S., and Weng, M.-H. (2021). 'Convergence of Public Participation, Participatory Design and NLP to Do-Develop Circular Economy', *Circular Economy and Sustainability*, 1, 917–934.

Dyer, T. (2014). 'Glass Recycling'. In *Handbook of Recycling*, pp. 191–209. Elsevier.

Hong Kong Institute for Monetary and Financial Research 2023.

EBF. (2022). 'Banking in Europe: EBF Facts & Figures 2022, European Banking Federation', https://www.ebf.eu/factsandfigures/.

European Parliament (EP). (2017). 'Circular Economy: Definition, Importance and Benefits', https://www.europarl.europa.eu/RegData/etudes/BRIE/2024/762852/EPRS_BRI(2024)762852_EN.pdf.

Esposito, M., Tse, T., and Soufani, K. (2018). 'Introducing a Circular Economy: New Thinking with New Managerial and Policy Implications', *California Management Review*, 60 (3), 5–19.

Fazey, I., Schäpke, N., Caniglia, G., Patterson, J., Hultman, J., van Mierlo, B., and Wiek, A. (2020). 'Transforming Knowledge Systems for Life on Earth: Visions of Future Systems and How to Get There', *Energy Research & Social Science*, 70, 101724, https://doi.org/10.1016/J.ERSS.2020.101724.

Fernandez, S., Jenkins, P., and Vieira, B. (2020). 'Europe's Digital Migration During COVID-19: Getting Past the Broad Trends and Averages', McKinsey, pp. 1–10, https://www.mckinsey.com/capabilities/mckinsey-digital/our-insights/europes-digital-migration-during-covid-19-getting-past-the-broad-trends-and-averages.

Friedman, M. (1991). *The Island of Stone Money*. Stanford, CA: Hoover Institution, Stanford University.

Furness, W. H. (1910). *The Island of Stone Money, UAP of the Carolines*. Philadelphia, PA: JB Lippincott.

Goda, K., and Kitsuregawa, M. (2012). 'The History of Storage Systems', *Proceedings of the IEEE*, 100 (6), 1433–1440, https://doi.org/10.1109/JPROC.2012.2189787.

Gomber, P., Kauffman, R. J., Parker, C., and Weber, B. W. (2018). 'On the FinTech Revolution: Interpreting the Forces of Innovation, Disruption, and Transformation in Financial Services', *Journal of Management Information Systems*, 35 (1), 220–265.

Hajro, N., Hjartar, K., Jenkins, P., and Vieira, B. (2021). 'What's Next for Digital Consumers', McKinsey, pp. 1–16. https://www.mckinsey.com/capabilities/mckinsey-digital/our-insights/whats-next-for-digital-consumers.

Hasan, K. K. (2021). 'Takas ekonomisinin zorlukları. Magellanique', https://www.magellanique.com/post/takas-ekonomisinin-zorluklar%C4%B1.

Hashimy, L., and Sandner, P. (2020). 'The Impact of Financial Regulation on the Development of Distributed Ledger Technology (DLT) Firms', *Frontiers in Blockchain*, 3, 21, https://doi.org/10.3389/fbloc.2020.00021.

Hilbert, M. (2020). 'Digital Technology and Social Change: The Digital Transformation of Society from a Historical Perspective'. *Dialogues in Clinical Neuroscience*, 22, 189–194.
https://doi.org/10.31887/DCNS.2020.22.2/mhilbert
Hong Kong Institute for Monetary and Financial Research. (2023). 'An Assessment on the Benefits of Bond Tokenisation', *SSRN Electronic Journal*.
https://efdata.org/.
https://www.climatebonds.net/2024/06/record-start-year-sustainable-debt.
https://www.researchgate.net/figure/World-population-growth-1700-2100-Courtesy-https-ourworldindataorg-Urban_fig1_346651495.
https://yesilbuyume.org/avrupa-yesil-mutabakati-ve-surdurulebilir-finans/.
International Committee for Museums and Collection of Glass (ICOM). (2021). *International Year of Glass 2022 (IYOG2022): The Global Glass Economy and Its Wider Social Consequences*. Berlin: International Commission on Glass.
Jevons, W. S. (1875). *Money and the Mechanism of Exchange*. New York: D. Appleton & Co.
King, B. (2018). *Bank 4.0: Banking Everywhere, Never at a Bank*. Hoboken, NJ: Wiley.
Khamitdkhanovich, N. A., Rajendran, M., Nailevich, I. R., and Krishnakumari, S. (2025). 'Green Finance and ESG Investing: Driving Sustainable Growth Through Innovation', *AIP Conference Proceedings*, 3306 (1), 030025.
Kirchherr, J., Reike, D., and Hekkert, M. (2017). 'Conceptualizing the Circular Economy: An Analysis of 114 Definitions', *Resources, Conservation and Recycling*, 127, 221–232.
Köksal, S. (2023). 'DLT in Treasury (1): Can Blockchain Improve the Deal Life Cycle With Smart Contracts? Medium', https://0xsemihkoksal.medium.com/dlt-in-treasury-1-can-blockchain-improve-the-deal-life-cycle-with-smart-contracts-69616ae142da.
KPMG. (2022). 'Digitalization in Banking Beyond COVID-19', pp. 1–16.
_____ (2023). 'Pulse of Fintech 2023: Global Trends in FinTech'.
Kraus, S., Burtscher, J., Vallaster, C., and Angerer, M. (2018). 'Sustainable Entrepreneurship Orientation: A Reflection on Status-Quo Research on Factors Facilitating Responsible Managerial Practices', *Sustainability*, 10 (2), 444, https://doi.org/10.3390/su10020444.
Kumar, S., Sharma, D., Rao, S., Lim, W. M., and Mangla, S. K. (2022). 'Past, Present, and Future of Sustainable Finance: Insights From Big

Data Analytics Through Machine Learning of Scholarly Research', *Annals of Operations Research*, 345, 1061–1104, https://doi.org/10.1007/s10479-021-04410-8.

Lenz, R. (2016). 'Peer-to-Peer Lending: Opportunities and Risks', *European Journal of Risk Regulation*, 7 (4), 688–700.

Lin, K.-Y. (2018). 'User Experience-Based Product Design for Smart Production to Empower Industry 4.0 in the Glass Recycling Circular Economy', *Computers & Industrial Engineering*, 125, 729–739.

Linnenluecke, M. K., Marrone, M., and Singh, A. K. (2020). 'Sixty Years of Accounting and Finance: A Bibliometric Analysis of Major Research Themes and Contributions', *Accounting and Finance*, 60 (4), 3217–3251, https://doi.org/10.1111/acfi.12714.

Liu, E. X. (2021). *Stay Competitive in the Digital Age: The Future of Banks*. IMF Working Paper, pp. 1–42.

Luo, W., Tian, Z., Zhong, S., Lyu, Q., and Deng, M. (2022). 'Global Evolution of Research on Sustainable Finance From 2000 to 2021: A Bibliometric Analysis on WoS Database', *Sustainability (Switzerland)*, 14 (15), 9435, https://doi.org/10.3390/su14159435.

MacArthur, E. (2013). *Towards the Circular Economy Vol. 1: An Economic and Business Rationale for an Accelerated Transition*. Cowes: Ellen MacArthur Foundation.

Malamas, V., Dasaklis, T., Arakelian, V., and Chondrokoukis, G. (2020). 'A Blockchain Framework for Increased Trust in Green Bonds Issuance', *Journal of Sustainable Finance & Investment*, forthcoming.

Malyshev, A. (2023). 'What Is Digital Banking? Meaning, Types and Benefits', SDK Finance, https://sdk.finance/what-is-digital-banking/, accessed 7 November 2023.

Martínez-Climent, C., Costa-Climent, R., and Oghazi, P. (2019). 'Sustainable Financing Through Crowdfunding', *Sustainability*, 11 (3), 934–950, https://doi.org/10.3390/su11030934.

Mbiti, I., and Weil, D. N. (2016). *Mobile Banking: The Impact of M-Pesa in Kenya*. NBER Working Paper Series, No. 17129. .

McKinsey. (2023). 'The Global Banking Annual Review 2023: The Great Banking Transition', https://www.mckinsey.com/industries/financial-services/our-insights/global-banking-annual-review.

Meloni, M., Souchet, F., and Sturges, D. (2018). *Circular Consumer Electronics: An Initial Exploration*. Cowes: Ellen MacArthur Foundation, pp. 1–17.

Murinde, V., Rizopoulos, E., and Zachariadis, M. (2022). 'The Impact of the FinTech Revolution on the Future of Banking: Opportunities and Risks', *International Review of Financial Analysis*, 81, 1–27.

Nakamoto, S. (2008). 'Bitcoin: A Peer-to-Peer Electronic Cash System', https://bitcoin.org/bitcoin.pdf, accessed 20 March 2026.

Namvar, A., and Naderpour, M. (2018). 'Handling Uncertainty in Social Lending Credit Risk Prediction With a Choquet Fuzzy Integral Model', *arXiv preprint*, arXiv:1804.10796.

Nar, M. (2019). 'Takas ekonomisinin doğuşu ve gelişimi', *Journal of Economy Culture and Society*, 60, 47–58, https://doi.org/10.26650/JECS2019-0006.

OECD. (2020). 'Digital Disruption in Banking and its Impact on Competition', http://www.oecd.org/daf/competition/digital-disruption-in-financial-markets.htm.

Param. (2020). 'Fintek Nedir? Fintek Tarihçesi ve Sunduğu Çözümler', https://blog.param.com.tr/fintek-nedir-finteklerin-gelecegi/.

Pearce, D. W., and Turner, R. K. (1989). *Economics of Natural Resources and the Environment*. Baltimore, MA: Johns Hopkins University Press.

Porfírio, J. A., Felício, J. A., and Carrilho, T. (2024). 'Factors Affecting Digital Transformation in Banking', *Journal of Business Research*, 171, 1–9.

Radhakrishnan, S. (2021). 'Circular Economy in Textiles and Fashion'. In *Circular Economy: Assessment and Case Studies*, pp. 163–202.

Ren, Y. S., Ma, C. Q., Chen, X. Q., Lei, Y. T., and Wang, Y. R. (2023). 'Sustainable Finance and Blockchain: A Systematic Review and Research Agenda', *Research in International Business and Finance*, 64, 101871, https://doi.org/10.1016/j.ribaf.2022.101871.

Rezende, C., de Carvalho Ferreira, M., Amorim Sobreiro, V., Kimura, H., de Moraes, L., and Barboza, F. (2016). 'A Systematic Review of Literature About Finance and Sustainability', *Journal of Sustainable Finance and Investment*, 6 (2), 112–147, https://doi.org/10.1080/20430795.2016.1177438.

Sadiku, A., Lesjak, D., Kohun, F., Pushavat, K., and Natek, S. (2022). 'Future of Traditional Banking and its Digitalization', *Issues in Information Systems*, 23 (3), 231–241.

Sariatli, F. (2017). 'Linear Economy Versus Circular Economy: A Comparative and Analyzer Study for Optimization of Economy for Sustainability', *Visegrad Journal on Bioeconomy and Sustainable Development*, 6 (1), 31–34.

Schandl, H., King, W., Kaksonen, A. H., Tapsuwan, S., and Baynes, T. M. (2020). 'National Circular Economy Roadmap for Plastics, Glass, Paper and Tires'.

Schueffel, P. (2016). 'Taming the Beast: A Scientific Definition of FinTech', *Journal of Innovation Management*, 4 (4), 32–54.

Singhania, M., Chadha, G., and Prasad, R. (2023). *Sustainable Finance Research: Review and Agenda*. Hoboken, NJ: Wiley, https://doi.org/10.1002/ijfe.28544.

Sreedevi, S. C., & Salahudeen, R. M. (2021). 'Sustainability Route for Industry 4.0: The Future of Global Circular Economic Transition'. In *Circular Economy-Recent Advances, New Perspectives and Applications*. IntechOpen..

Statista. (2023). 'Number of Digital Payment Users Worldwide From 2017 to 2025', https://www.statista.com/statistics/number-of-digital-payment-users

Su, B., Heshmati, A., Geng, Y., and Yu, X. (2013). 'A Review of the Circular Economy in China: Moving From Rhetoric to Implementation', *Journal of Cleaner Production*, 42, 215–227.

Suri, T., and Jack, W. (2016). 'The Long-Run Poverty and Gender Impacts of Mobile Money', *Science*, 354 (6317), 1288–1292.

Şimşek, C. M., Özkan, C., and Gürgün, G. (2024). 'Cyclical Analysis on Sustainable and Green Financial Instruments: Review Article', *Balkan Journal of Social Sciences*, 13 (25), 29–40.

Tao, H., Zhuang, S., Xue, R., Cao, W., Tian, J., and Shan, Y. (2022). 'Environmental Finance: An Interdisciplinary Review', *Technological Forecasting and Social Change*, 179, 121639, https://doi.org/10.1016/j.techfore.2022.121639.

Tran, P. T. T., Le, T. T. H., and Phan, N. H. T. (2023). 'Digital Transformation of the Banking Industry in Developing Countries', *International Journal of Professional Business Review*, 8 (5), 1–24.

Türkiye Blockchain Platformu. (2024). 'Tokenizasyon: Geleceğin para ve varlık sistemi (s. 6). Finans, Bankacılık ve Sigortacılık Çalışma Grubu', https://bctr.org/wp-content/uploads/2024/01/tokenizasyon_rapor_230124_compressed.pdf.

UN, United Nations Environment Programme. (2018). 'SDG 12 Issue Brief: Ensuring Sustainable Consumption and Production Patterns'.

UNCTAD. (2022). 'Impact of COVID -19 Pandemic on Trade and Development Lessons Learned', https:// unctad.org/publication/impact-covid-19-pandemic-trade-and-development-lessons-learned.

Wang, H., and Yu, S. (2021). 'Robo-Advising: Enhancing Investment With Inverse Optimization and Deep Reinforcement Learning', *arXiv preprint*, arXiv:2105.09264.

World Bank. (2018). *The Global Findex Database 2017: Measuring Financial Inclusion and the FinTech Revolution*. Washington, DC: World Bank Publications.

_____ (2021). *World Development Report 2021*. Washington, DC: World Bank Publications.

_____ (2021). *World Development Report 2021: Data for Better Lives*. Washington, DC: World Bank Publications.

Wright, T. (2020). 'The Berkeley Blockchain Initiative—Crypto Municipal Bonds: Addressing the Challenge of Homelessness and a Whole Lot More'. In *CrowdAsset: Crowdfunding for Policymakers*, pp. 471–477. .

Yang, Y., Chow, A. L. H., and Golubchik, L. (2008). *'Multi-Torrent: A Performance Study'. In Proceedings of the 2008 IEEE International Symposium on Modeling, Analysis and Simulation of Computers and Telecommunication Systems*, IEEE.

List of Contributors

Sonat Bayram, Asst. Prof., Cyprus Health and Social Sciences University

Serkan Yeşilyurt, Asst. Prof. Dr., Bahcesehir University, Faculty of Economics, Administrative and Social Sciences, Department of Economics

Çağlar Yurtseven, Prof. Dr., Bahcesehir University, Faculty of Applied Sciences, Faculty of Economics, Administrative and Social Sciences, Department of Economics

Didem Cicerali, Res. Assist. Bahcesehir University, Faculty of Applied Sciences, Economy

Gökhan Sönmezler, Prof. Dr., Trakya University, Faculty of Applied Sciences, Finance and Banking

Semih Köksal, Banking Treasure Specialist

İsmail Orçun Gündüz, Prof. Dr., Trakya University, Faculty of Applied Sciences, Finance and Banking